CULTURES OF THE WORLD

NETHERLANDS

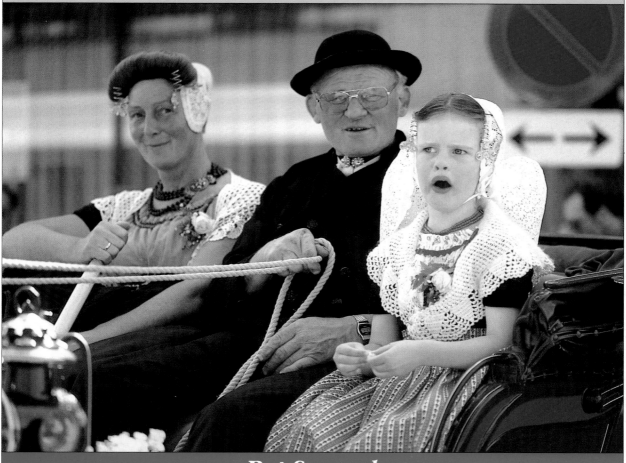

Pat Seward

MARSHALL CAVENDISH
New York • London • Sydney

Reference edition published 1995 by
Marshall Cavendish Corporation
2415 Jerusalem Avenue
P.O. Box 587
North Bellmore
New York 11710

© Times Editions Pte Ltd 1995

Originated and designed by
Times Books International, an imprint of
Times Editions Pte Ltd

Printed in Singapore

Library of Congress Cataloging-in-Publication Data:
Seward, Pat.
   Netherlands / Pat Seward
     p. cm.—(Cultures Of The World)
   Includes bibliographical references and index.
   ISBN 0-7614-0171-7 (Netherlands)
   ISBN 0-7614-0167-9 (Set)
   1. Netherlands—Juvenile works. [1. Netherlands] I. Title.
II. Series.
DJ18.S49 1995
949.2—dc20   94–43352
             CIP
              AC

Cultures of the World

Editorial Director	Shirley Hew
Managing Editor	Shova Loh
Editors	Elizabeth Berg
	Dinah Lee
	Azra Moiz
	Sue Sismondo
Picture Editor	Susan Jane Manuel
Production	Anthoney Chua
Design	Tuck Loong
	Felicia Wong
	Loo Chuan Ming
	Wendy Koh
Illustrators	Chow Kok Keong
	Anuar bin Abdul Rahim
MCC Editorial Director	Evelyn M. Fazio

INTRODUCTION

THE GEOGRAPHICAL LOCATION of the Netherlands has been the decisive factor in shaping its development, the character of its people, and their culture. The country is dominated by water—from three great rivers and the North Sea. For centuries the Dutch have fought the sea, losing land at one point only to win it back at another. Nearly half the area of the country is below sea level, and a large proportion of the land was created by the Dutch.

At the same time, the sea and the rivers have presented the Dutch with trading opportunities, which they have carefully nurtured. The navigable rivers allowed them to trade with their huge hinterland in continental Europe, and the sea on their doorstep enabled them to open markets across the world. Through diligent trade abroad and careful housekeeping at home, this small country has achieved a world influence out of all proportion to its size and population.

CONTENTS

A Dutch woman in traditional headdress from Edam.

CONTENTS

The Netherlands has long been known as the florist of Europe. For the Dutch, "Tulips from Amsterdam" and other flowers and bulbs are major money-earners.

GEOGRAPHY

IT IS SAID IN THE NETHERLANDS that the Lord created the land, except for Holland, which was created by the Dutch. The history, economy, and character of the Dutch people have been strongly influenced by their continuous battle with water—the sea and the rivers that flow through their low-lying land.

The country is officially known as the Netherlands, but it is often called "Holland." Strictly this name only applies to the two provinces of North and South Holland, which border the North Sea in the Amsterdam-The Hague area. The name for those who live in the Netherlands is "the Dutch," a word which also describes their language. The name Netherlands comes from the word *neder*, meaning "low" and *lands*, meaning "countries." For this reason, the Netherlands is also called the Low Countries.

The Netherlands—a little larger than Maryland and a little smaller than West Virginia—is one of the smaller countries of northern Europe. It is situated at the mouth of the Rhine, where the great river, which rises 820 miles (1320 km) away in the Alps, finally flows into the North Sea. To the east the Netherlands is bordered by Germany and to the south by Belgium. To the north and west, the North Sea is an ever-present threat.

The Kingdom of the Netherlands today also includes the Netherlands Antilles in the Caribbean. These islands include Aruba, Curaçao, and Bonaire in the western Leeward Islands, and St. Eustatius, Saba, and St. Maarten in the northern Leeward Islands.

Opposite: **For hundreds of years, windmills drained the low-lying land and opened up areas for agriculture and settlement.**

Above: **A dike formed by raised land. Dunes and dikes protect low-lying areas that would otherwise be flooded by the sea. Without dikes, about one-third of the country would be flooded.**

DIFFERENT REGIONS

Much of the Netherlands consists of land reclaimed from the sea over the past seven or eight hundred years, and a great deal of the total area—about one-third—is therefore below sea level, with the lowest point, near Rotterdam, 22 feet (6.7 m) below. More than half the country is less than 16 feet (4.8 m) above sea level and, because of the presence of large lakes such as the IJsselmeer ("EH-sul-meer"), only five-sixths of the country is dry land.

The low-lying western coastal region is characterized by *polders* ("POHL-der"), dikes, canals, and lakes. A polder is an area of reclaimed land, often below sea level, inside a dike or wall constructed to keep the sea from flooding in. Polders can be many square miles in area and often contain towns and villages, in addition to large expanses of farmland. Many Dutch cities, including Amsterdam and The Hague, are built on polders.

Most of the Netherlands' landscape is totally flat. Canals drain the polder region. About 40% of the Netherlands' land area consists of polders. The polder region is also the country's main farming region.

Most lakes are found in the polder region. The Netherlands' largest lake is the IJsselmeer. In 1932, the Dutch dammed the Zuiderzee ("ZOU-der-zay"), originally an inlet of the North Sea. A 19-mile (30-km) barrier dam was built linking the provinces of North Holland and Friesland ("FREES-land"). Over the years, the resulting lake, IJsselmeer, has become freshwater because of the continuous fresh water flow from the IJssel river. Friesland—a farming province with its own distinct language—lies to the north of IJsselmeer. Parts of the lake have also been reclaimed to form a new province called Flevoland ("FLAY-voh-land").

Along the southwest coast, the Schelde ("SGHEL-duh"), Waal, and Maas

NETHERLANDS

Feet
656
0
200
0 Lowlands

0 30 Miles
0 30 Kilometers

Land reclaimed from Zuiderzee

WEST FRISIAN ISLANDS

Waddenzee

Barrier Dam

TEXEL
ISLAND

NORTH SEA

Lake I Jssel
(Zuiderzee)

North Sea Canal MARKEN I.

Amsterdam

Amstel R.

Loosdrecht
Lakes

I Jssel R.

Rotterdam

Lower Rhine R.

Hook of Holland

Canal

Lek

R.

Nieuwe
Maas R.

Waal R.

GERMANY

DELTA

East Schelde

REGION

West Schelde

Maas R.

Rhine R.

Schelde R.

BELGIUM

Vaalser
Mtn. (1,053 feet, 322 meters)

Much of the country consists of land reclaimed from the sea over the past 700 to 800 years. From the 13th century to the present, the Dutch have reclaimed over 2,700 square miles (7,000 sq km) of land. A large proportion of this—about 2,400 square miles (6,200 sq km)—has been reclaimed by means of coastal dikes.

rivers form a complex river delta. This delta province, Zeeland (meaning "land of the sea"), has always been vulnerable to flooding.

Over many centuries, sand deposited by the sea has built up dunes along the coastline, resulting in the string of low-lying Frisian Islands. These enclose the Waddenzee ("WAH-den-zay") and protect the coast from flooding. The waters here are seldom more than 10 feet (3 m) deep even at high tide, and it is possible to walk from the mainland to the islands across the mud flats at low tide.

The inner parts of the country are at higher altitudes than the polder region, but these provinces are not as well drained by rivers. Inland areas, such as Limburg province and the region along the German border, have sandy heath and low hills. The highest point, Vaalser at 1,053 feet (322 meters), is in the far southeast where the Dutch, German, and Belgian borders meet.

THE POWER IN THE WIND

Were it not for the windmill, Holland as we know it would not exist today. For more than 600 years, the Dutch have used windmills to drain their land and keep it dry. Wherever one looks, there are windmills of one kind or another: small meadow mills in the fields, mills standing on artificial hills, mills with external stages or balconies, brick mills, wooden mills, and thatched mills. It is almost impossible to travel any significant distance without seeing either the chunky traditional mill with its broad sails, or its modern descendant—the tall wind turbine with its shining blades spinning in the breeze.

Although they were primarily used for drainage in their heyday, windmills also performed many other tasks. Initially, they were probably developed for grinding grains such as wheat and corn, then for spices, paint, and flint for pottery. In 1592, Cornelis Cornelisz built the first wind-powered sawmill. Other types of mill were developed to pulp wood for the production of paper, for the extraction of linseed and rapeseed oil, and for pounding hemp.

The earliest mills were post mills, in which all the moving parts—the sails, the gearing, and the millstones—were contained in a squarish, hut-like structure that turned on a central vertical post. Interior wooden gears, such as those shown here, turned the sails. Access to the cramped interior was by means of a short ladder at the rear of the mill. Generally, post mills and their close relatives the wip mills, with their rectangular mill houses and pyramid-shaped bases, were quite small. Their size tended to limit their uses to grinding corn and pumping water. Nevertheless, they were constructed in the hundreds, and they can still be seen in significant numbers today.

Since windmills were such a visible and important part of the landscape, they were also used for sending messages. Sails that were set at vertical and horizontal meant that the mill was ready to start work; if the sails were at 45 degrees to the ground, the windmill could not work. News of a birth was signaled by the sails being set at before 6 and 12 o'clock; deaths were signaled by sails set after 6 and 12 o'clock. On special occasions, the sails were decorated with baskets, tin hearts, garlands or flowers, and angels.

The names of the people who built these windmills, so essential to Dutch life, are still remembered. In addition, each windmill has its own name, which can be seen painted on the head, just below the point where the sails are attached. A visitor might see "Goliath," with "The Four Winds" and "de Jonge Hendrik" a little farther on. The English word "gang" is said to come from a Dutch word meaning a group of windmills working together.

The days when the windmill played an active role in Dutch life have long since passed. By the end of the World War I, the windmill as a serious source of industrial power was effectively dead. At one time, the Netherlands could boast between nine and ten thousand active windmills, but their small capacity, their vulnerability to fire and wind damage, and the increasing availability of better sources of power meant that they could not survive. In recent times, their function has been taken over by the electric motor and the electric pump.

In the 1990s barely 1,000 windmills remain, but they are popular tourist attractions in both the Dutch countryside and the towns. One of the major sights of the Rotterdam area, for instance, is the complex of large drainage mills along the Kinderdijk ("KIN-der-dayk") (shown below). At the other end of the scale, many replicas and models of windmills are found in the gardens of suburban homes.

RECLAIMING THE LAND

Land reclamation takes place in distinct stages. First, dikes are built around the area to be reclaimed. Then, water in the enclosed area is pumped out until dry land—the polder—starts to appear. To keep this polder dry, a network of small canals is constructed to drain the water into collector canals. From here the water is pumped to canals outside and above the polder, to be carried to the sea. Because rain and sea or river water continually seep into the polder, pumping has to be maintained every day.

Even after the surface has dried out, it is still unsuitable for agriculture due to the salt residue left by the sea. Coarse grass is then planted and left to grow for a few years; this slowly eliminates the salt and helps to bind the soil together. Rain and continuous pumping further remove all traces of salt. Finally, the land is turned over to agriculture and settlement.

One of the largest reclamation projects in this century occurred after the damming of the Zuiderzee in 1932. Once this was turned into a large inland lake, four large polders were reclaimed and drained: the Wieringermeer, North-East, South Flevoland, and East Flevoland polders. These four polders have increased the country's land area by about 407,000 acres (165,000 hectares).

THE GREAT STORM OF 1953

Since the Netherlands is especially vulnerable to flooding by the sea, this poses a real danger to its people, 60% of whom live in low-lying parts. Although the many canals, dams, dikes, and pumping stations work around the clock to prevent flooding, these are not always effective.

On the night of January 31, 1953, a disastrous storm combined with high tides and gale force winds brought the North Sea sweeping over the sea defenses. The notorious North Sea surge breached dikes and barriers, and swept over the entire province of Zeeland and large parts of North Brabant and South Holland. Over 1,800 people were drowned, along with tens of thousands of farm animals. More than 130 towns were destroyed and almost 50,000 homes were flooded.

Damage to buildings and land ran into hundreds of millions of Dutch guilders. About 400,000 acres (162,000 hectares) of land was flooded. Hard-won agricultural land was contaminated by salt, large areas of the southwest disappeared under the waves, and the sea water even reached Rotterdam's suburbs, about 25 miles (40 km) from the sea.

THE DELTA PROJECT

The Delta Project in Zeeland province was devised to prevent any further disasters like the 1953 flood. The plan envisaged the construction of a series of dams across the many mouths of the Rhine and Schelde rivers, and between the low islands facing the North Sea.

Three artificial islands were constructed on existing sandbanks to seal off the estuaries from the sea. However, many people objected to the enclosing of what they regarded as a unique and beautiful area, and there was also pressure to allow commercial fishing to continue. Eventually an open dam or storm-surge barrier was built across the Eastern Schelde— 2 miles (3.2 km) long with 65 concrete piers, between which 62 steel gates are suspended. These vertical gates normally remain open but can be lowered to keep out the sea when flood conditions threaten. Dams and secondary dikes were also built in other parts of Zeeland province.

The storm-surge barrier in the Eastern Schelde, Zeeland. In this low-lying land, high tides and strong winds are a constant threat and have broken flood barriers, causing serious loss of life and land.

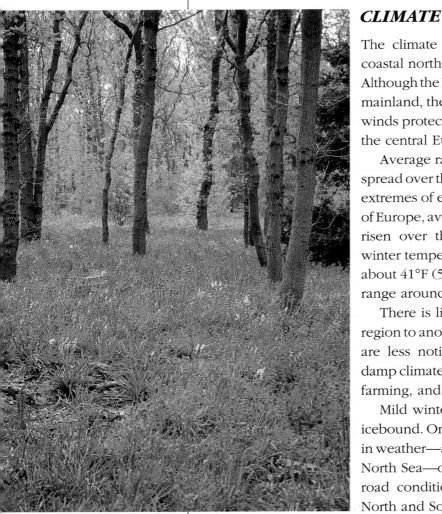

Bluebells bloom in the woods in springtime.

CLIMATE

The climate in the Netherlands is typical of coastal northern Europe—mild, wet, and cool. Although the Netherlands is part of the European mainland, the Gulf Stream and the westerly sea winds protect the country from the extremes of the central European winter.

Average rainfall is 30 inches (76 cm) evenly spread over the year. Temperatures rarely reach extremes of either hot or cold. As in other parts of Europe, average temperatures have gradually risen over the past 200 years. The average winter temperature in Amsterdam in January is about 41°F (5°C). Summer temperatures in July range around 69°F (21°C).

There is little variation in climate from one region to another, although the maritime effects are less noticeable farther inland. The mild, damp climate supports grasslands and livestock farming, and favors horticulture.

Mild winters mean that shipping is seldom icebound. On the other hand, frequent changes in weather—another result of being close to the North Sea—often give rise to fog and slippery road conditions in winter. The flat areas of North and South Holland facing the North Sea are very windy, and as a result, wind turbine farms for the production of electricity are frequently sited in this region.

FLORA AND FAUNA

The Netherlands is such a crowded country that wildlife has to fit in wherever it can. Wildlife mainly takes the form of birds, fish, and small rather than large animals.

Special areas have been created to protect flowers and trees, wildlife, and natural habitats. Hawks, cormorants, swans, ducks, and geese abound in these sanctuaries, as do small mammals such as squirrels. In addition, wading birds can be found in large numbers on the mud flats at the mouths of the many rivers. Foxes, boar, red deer, and the dormouse are found in the higher provinces.

The grey heron is a wading bird that is found in mudflats near polders and estuarine regions.

Land reclamation and the construction of dams have had an adverse effect on birds, marine creatures, and coastal flora. Most early dams were solid, except for a few with locks to serve coastal shipping. Although solid dams were effective in protecting the coastline, they had certain disadvantages, especially for species of birds that depend for their food on the continual covering and uncovering of mud banks formed by the tide. Another problem was that the dammed lakes slowly lost their salt content, and there were fears for the well-being of both the oyster population and the fishers who depended on them for their living.

As time passed, however, it became apparent that oysters were able to cope with the new tideless conditions. As for the wading birds, when these left, other birds, notably flamingos, moved in to take their place. Nature adapted to the new conditions, but the Dutch authorities still receive many complaints from environmentalists about the long- and short-term effects of the dams.

TOWNS AND SETTLEMENTS

The densest concentration of population in the Netherlands is found in the Randstad ("ROHN-stadt" meaning Rim City). This stretches from Amsterdam to Rotterdam and includes the towns of Haarlem, Leiden, The Hague, and Utrecht ("OOH-trekht").

AMSTERDAM The capital of the Netherlands, Amsterdam straddles the IJ ("EH") and Amstel rivers and is named after a dam on the Amstel river. The city is surrounded by a network of canals and bordered by tall, elegant buildings. It has a population of 713,000.

In the 16th century, Amsterdam became the main center of economic prosperity in the Netherlands and, in the 19th century, it also became the diamond center of the world.

Schiphol ("SHIP-hol") airport, south of the city, is one of the most important hub airports in Europe. The tourist industry has added to Amsterdam's importance. Amsterdam's progressive attitude can be seen in its legal red light district and the lenient attitude toward the use of soft drugs.

Among Amsterdam's most famous features are its *grachtengordel* ("GRACH-ten-GHOR-del"), three canals that fan out in a concentric circle: the Herengracht, the Keizersgracht, and the Prinsengracht.

THE HAGUE Although it is not the capital of the Netherlands, the government and administration of the country is in The Hague. The city's official name is 's Gravenhage ("SGRAH-ven-HAH-geh"), but it is commonly called Den Haag ("dun HAAGH") by the Dutch. International organizations such as the International Court of Justice (part of the United Nations) and the International Institute of Social Studies are located in The Hague, which has a population of 445,000.

ROTTERDAM Rotterdam is the second largest city in the Netherlands and the world's largest port. It lies on the Nieuwe Maas river about 19 miles (30 km) from the North Sea, and has a population of 590,000. Rotterdam is connected to the industrial heartland of Europe by an extensive system of canals linked to the Rhine River.

During World War II, Rotterdam was almost entirely destroyed by both German and Allied bombing raids, but it has since been completely rebuilt.

UTRECHT The third largest city in the Netherlands, Utrecht is an ancient city dating back to Roman times. The city's university was founded in 1636 and is the second oldest in the country. The Old Canal snakes through the city center well below street level. Utrecht's industries produce a variety of manufactured goods. It has a population of 234,000.

MAASTRICHT Maastricht was initially a Roman town guarding an important crossing of the Maas river. Due to its proximity to Belgium and Germany, it is a cosmopolitan city with its own dialect, a diverse architectural style, and a rich international cuisine. Maastricht is largely Catholic, in contrast to the Protestant north. Today, the town is an important trading and industrial center specializing in ceramics, papermaking, and cement. It has a population of 118,000.

AAN PRINS WILLEM DEN EERSTEN
D
KONING W   TWEEDEN
T   D.

HISTORY

THE HISTORY OF THE NETHERLANDS has been connected for the past 2,000 years with that of its neighbors, Belgium and Luxembourg. For many centuries, these three countries were known collectively as the Low Countries.

FOREIGN INVASIONS

The Netherlands has been invaded and occupied by foreign powers for much of its history. From the first to the fourth centuries A.D., the Romans occupied the Low Countries, together with Celtic tribes such as the Batavi and the Frisians. The Frisians are believed to have pioneered the building of dikes. Over 2,000 years ago, they built mounds of earth along the marshy coast of Friesland to keep the sea out.

From the fifth century onward, the Germanic Saxons and Franks occupied most of the country, except for the lands held by the Frisians. In the eighth century Charlemagne, a Frankish king, incorporated the Low Countries into his Holy Roman Empire, and in the ninth century Vikings from Scandinavia made the Utrecht area one of their bases for further raiding.

For the next two hundred years, the Low Countries were the subject of continuous feuding and division by armies. Then slowly, between the 10th and 13th centuries, the provinces that we now see on the map were carved out and stabilized by a succession of princes, bishops, and counts. From the 14th to the 16th centuries, the Low Countries came under a succession of foreign rulers—the French Burgundians, the Austrian Hapsburgs, and the Spanish.

Opposite: **Statue of William II of Orange in The Hague.**

Above: **A coat of arms at Kasteeltuinen in Arcen, Limburg.**

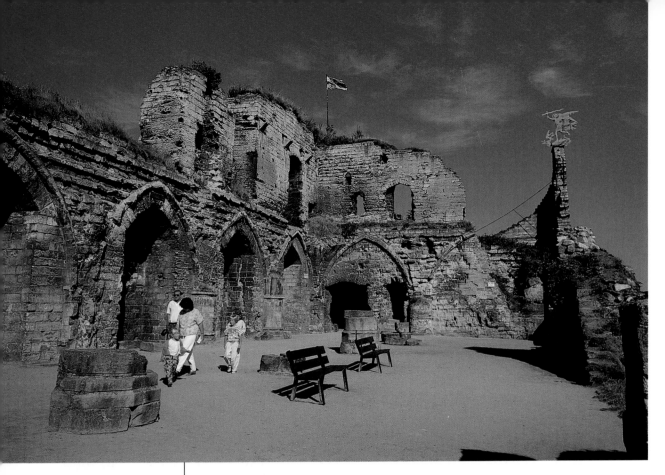

Ruins at Valkenburg castle in Limburg province date back almost 1,000 years.

THE MIDDLE AGES

During the Middle Ages, the area now known as the Netherlands was split into a number of autonomous duchies and counties in addition to land ruled by the Bishop of Utrecht. The French Burgundians controlled northern France and what is now Belgium, and in the late 14th century their power stretched to the present provinces of Limburg and Brabant. In the 15th century, this was extended to Holland, Zeeland, and Gelderland.

In 1477 Mary, daughter and heir of the duke of Burgundy, married into the Hapsburg family of Austria, and as a result the Low Countries came under Hapsburg control. Mary's son, Philip, later married into the Spanish royal family, and Philip's son, Charles, inherited the Spanish throne. In 1515, Charles I of Spain inherited the Low Countries from his father, and acquired the remaining Dutch provinces. The Low Countries were nominally Catholic, although Amsterdam was tolerant of Protestants and became the focus of much Protestant inward migration.

DUTCH REVOLT

With the spread of Protestantism in Europe, Charles became more concerned by the Protestant revolt, and strict Catholicism was imposed on Amsterdam. In 1555, Charles abdicated in favor of his son, Philip II. Philip was a devout Catholic who condemned thousands of Dutch Protestants to death for heresy.

He sent the Duke of Alva to restore Catholic control of Amsterdam in 1567. However, the Dutch did not take kindly to being given orders by Philip, a distant, foreign king who had been born and brought up in Spain. In 1568, Prince William of Orange raised an army to fight the Spanish. This marked the beginning of the 80 Years' War of Independence. Although the war was about religion, Philip also wanted to limit the rapidly expanding Dutch economy, which threatened Spanish interests.

By 1572 William had captured Zeeland and Holland, and in 1573 he defeated the Duke of Alva's army in a battle at Zuiderzee. Although both the Dutch Catholics and Protestants joined forces to fight the Spanish, they remained divided about religion. The northern Dutch provinces were largely Protestant, whereas the south was mainly Catholic.

In 1581, seven northern provinces signed the Union of Utrecht treaty, under which they declared themselves the independent United Provinces of the Netherlands. The southern provinces—present-day Belgium and Luxembourg—remained under Spanish Catholic domination. However, Spain continued its land and sea attacks to regain control of the northern provinces. The 80 Years' War of Independence came to an end in 1648, when Spain finally recognized the Netherlands' independence.

The tomb of William of Orange at Delft. Nicknamed William the Silent for his ability to be discreet, he is remembered as the father of the nation. After winning independence, William was appointed the *stadhouder* ("STADT-how-der"), or governor, in 1579. He was assassinated by the Spanish in 1584.

THE GOLDEN AGE

A house in Amsterdam dating back to the 17th century. As Amsterdam flourished as the most important commercial center in Europe, its residents constructed many imposing buildings that still survive today.

Due to their location at the lower reaches of the Rhine, the United Provinces controlled the shipping that used this major river. Amsterdam began to prosper as a port, and the stage was set for Dutch adventurers to explore Asia and the Americas and to open up new areas for trade.

In the 17th century, Dutch merchants established trading posts all over the world, from the Far East to the Caribbean. The Dutch East India Company (*Vereenigde Oost-Indische Compagnie* or the VOC) was founded in Amsterdam in 1602 to handle trade between the United Provinces and territories in the Indian Ocean. The Dutch West India Company was established in 1621 to trade with the Americas and Africa. As commerce expanded, the United Provinces became extremely wealthy.

In parallel with the new prosperity and the religious toleration shown by the Dutch, spiritual and cultural life also flourished. This Golden Age produced many of the greatest Dutch painters—particularly Rembrandt, Vermeer, Frans Hals, and Ruysdael.

The Golden Age was also notable for a flowering in the arts of furniture-making, gold and silversmithing, and architecture. Scientific advances were also made—Antoni van Leeuwenhoek invented the microscope and studied microbiology.

BOURTANGE

Bourtange ("boor-TANG-eh"), in the northeastern Netherlands near the German border, is one of many fortified towns that played a vital role in protecting the United Provinces.

The town was built in 1593 on the orders of William of Orange. Its defenses included a star-shaped network of lakes and canals. At its heart was a central square, from which streets led directly to the various bastions within the protective moat. Outlook posts on every corner could give warning of the approach of the enemy.

Spanish forces besieged the town in the same year that it was built but without success. In 1672, a marauding German army captured 28 cities and entrenchments in northern Netherlands and demanded the surrender of Bourtange. The town's governor, Captain Prott, putting his trust in the surrounding marshes and in the well-tried defenses of the fortress, refused. The story is told that the Germans offered Prott 200,000 guilders to surrender, but he replied that he had an equal number of bullets for his foe. As a result of Prott's defiant response, Bourtange was attacked, but the German army eventually suffered a crushing defeat and withdrew.

CONTINUING WARS

The Netherlands' prosperity led to wars with other European countries—wars with the British and French, continuing struggle with Spain, and opportunist forays by the Germans.

The Dutch and British went to war twice over control of the sea. In the First Anglo-Dutch War, the Dutch Admiral van Tromp was forced to yield, but in 1667 Admiral de Ruyter made an audacious raid into the River Medway, near London. It was the only time that foreign guns have been heard in the British capital.

The War of the Spanish Succession, which broke out at the turn of the 18th century and dragged on for 12 years, drained Dutch finances and led indirectly to the end of the Golden Age.

CONQUERING A WIDER WORLD

The 17th century saw a rapid expansion of Dutch interests overseas, as explorers braved the unknown to open up trading routes and new settlements. As the result of an embargo on Dutch trade with Spain and Portugal, the Dutch turned their attention to direct trade with the East.

In 1596, Cornelis de Houtman arrived in Java and established Dutch occupation in the Indonesian archipelago. Batavia (now Jakarta, capital of Indonesia) was established by Jan Pieterzoon Coen in 1619 and became the administrative center of the colony. Known as the Dutch East Indies, it remained a Dutch colony until 1949, when it became independent.

Dutch adventurers and traders explored the world in their sailing ships. In 1596, William Barents discovered Spitzbergen in the Arctic Ocean while searching for a northeast route to India. New Zealand was discovered by another Dutch sailor, Abel Tasman, who also gave his name to the island of Tasmania in Australia. The Cape Colony, now Cape Town in South Africa, was founded by Jan van Riebeek in 1652 as a stopping point on the route to India.

In South America, the Guinea coast was occupied by the Dutch in 1613. Ten years later, parts of Brazil also became a Dutch colony. In North America, Nieuw Amsterdam was founded in 1625, and 20 years later Peter Stuyvesant became its last Dutch governor. By 1634, the Dutch also had a string of small possessions in the Antilles in the eastern Caribbean, many of which are still part of the Netherlands Antilles today.

FRENCH REVOLUTION AND AFTER

The Dutch remained independent for 150 years, until the rise of the French Empire in Napoleonic times. After a French army occupied the United Provinces in 1795, the conquered territory was renamed the Batavian Republic and became a vassal state of the French Empire. In 1806, Napoleon Bonaparte installed his brother Louis as king of Holland, and in 1810 the country was annexed to France.

The French occupation ended in 1814, when the Kingdom of the Netherlands came into being. This comprised the present-day Netherlands, Belgium, and Luxembourg. Unlike the previous republican system of government, where a *stadhouder,* or governor, ruled the country, the Netherlands became a constitutional monarchy under King William I, a descendant of Prince William of Orange.

A statue of Queen Wilhelmina.

During the 19th century, parliament became stronger as the sovereign's powers were slowly curbed. In 1814, a new constitution decreed that the monarch should govern and that ministers should be accountable to the sovereign. The constitution of 1848, which is still in force today, made ministers accountable to an elected parliament.

In 1839, the southern Catholic provinces of the Netherlands gained independence and became the country of Belgium. Luxembourg became independent in 1890, when Wilhelmina became queen of the Netherlands. On account of an ancient law that prevented women from ruling the grand duchy, Luxembourg could not recognize Wilhelmina as monarch and ended its union with the Netherlands.

WORLD WARS AND GERMAN OCCUPATION

A monument in Dam Square, Amsterdam, commemorating Dutch victims of World War Ii.

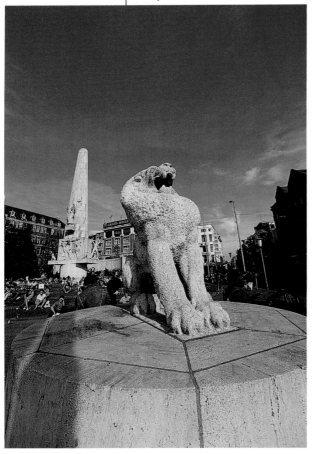

Although the Netherlands remained neutral during World War I, its merchant navy was taken over by allied forces and suffered attacks by the Germans. In World War II, the Netherlands was invaded by Germany in May 1940. After the destruction of Rotterdam by bombing, the Dutch capitulated in the face of Germany's overwhelming military power. Queen Wilhelmina and the Dutch government set up a government-in-exile in England, and Princess Juliana went to Canada with her family for safety.

German occupation of the Netherlands lasted five years and inflicted misery, humiliation, and degradation on the population. Food shortages, lack of freedom, forced labor, censorship, and curfews were common, and the deportation of Dutch Jews to concentration camps deprived the country of a well-integrated and vigorous minority. A Dutch resistance movement soon sprang up, but the Germans retaliated with random killings after each act of defiance.

Unfortunately for the Dutch, a bold plan by the Allies to bring the war to a swift end in September 1944 failed. The "Bridge too far" operation—a plan to capture the Arnhem bridge over the Rhine and isolate German troops—was a disaster. In the terrible winter that followed, thousands of Dutch died of starvation. Many were reduced to eating tulip bulbs to survive.

By April 1945, the Allies had liberated the Netherlands, and food and other supplies poured in to relieve the suffering. By the time the Germans officially surrendered on May 5, 1945, cities were in ruins, the economy was wrecked, and the population was at starvation point. Queen Wilhelmina and her government-in-exile returned to pick up the pieces and started the long task of reconstruction.

END OF EMPIRE

Until World War II, the Netherlands held colonies in Southeast Asia, the Caribbean, and South America, but these territories sought independence after 1945. After fierce fighting, the Netherlands was forced in 1949 to recognize the independence of its colonies in Southeast Asia, which later formed the Republic of Indonesia. By the 1954 Charter for the Kingdom, Surinam and the Netherlands Antilles (Aruba, Curaçao, Bonaire, St. Eustatius, Saba, and St. Maarten) in the eastern Caribbean became equal partners with the Netherlands, although the Netherlands remain responsible for defense and foreign policy. Surinam became independent in 1975, while the Netherlands Antilles have shared equal status with the Netherlands since 1986.

Tombstone of a Dutch colonialist in Malacca, Malaysia dating back to 1656. The Dutch captured Malacca from the Portuguese in 1641 and governed it until 1824, when the British took over.

THE NETHERLANDS TODAY

For centuries, Dutch foreign policy has been dictated by the geographical location of the Netherlands. Dependence on international trade has led the Dutch to take a particular interest in international law. This is evidenced by the number of international treaties signed in the Netherlands and the fact that the International Court of Justice is located in The Hague.

International Court of Justice at the Peace Palace in The Hague.

Dutch foreign policy since 1945 has focused on the pursuit of peace, stability, and a more just distribution of power and prosperity in the world. For this reason, the Netherlands is a member of many international organizations, such as the United Nations, the North Atlantic Treaty Organization (NATO), the Organization for Economic Cooperation and Development (OECD), and the Benelux Customs Union (together with Belgium and Luxembourg). Dutch support for disarmament, human rights, and the elimination of racial discrimination is widely respected.

In recent years, the Netherlands has also been a major force for the economic and political unification of Europe.

THE EUROPEAN UNION

The Netherlands is a founding member of the European Common Market, now known as the European Economic Community (EEC). The EEC was set up in 1958 to facilitate the free trade of goods and services among member countries. Initially there were six members—Belgium, West Germany, France, Italy, Luxembourg, and the Netherlands. In 1973, Britain, Ireland, and Denmark joined the organization. In 1980, they were followed by Greece, and by Spain and Portugal in 1986. By 1995, the existing membership of 12 countries will rise to 16 with the entry of Austria, Finland, Norway, and Sweden.

In late 1991, when the Netherlands held the presidency of the European Community, it promoted the Maastricht Treaty, which looks forward to the evolution of a supranational federal Europe, including full monetary union with a common currency and the removal of all trade barriers.

The Binnenhof complex in The Hague is the center of the Netherlands' government.

The Maastricht Treaty created the European Union, which incorporates the EEC, the European Coal and Steel Community, and the European Atomic Energy Commission. The Union came into being on November 1, 1993 and is, in effect, an enlarged and more powerful EEC with a common foreign and security policy and an agreement to cooperate on justice and home affairs issues.

GOVERNMENT

THE NETHERLANDS IS A REPUBLIC with a constitutional monarch. Although most Dutch people are fiercely democratic in outlook, the country has a widely respected hereditary monarch.

PARLIAMENT

The Dutch parliament is called the States General, a term left over from feudal times, when representatives of various estates were summoned by their lords to discuss political and financial matters. The States General has two chambers—a Lower and an Upper House.

The Lower House has 150 members, who are directly elected by the population for a four-year term. Universal male suffrage was introduced in 1917. Women were given the vote two years later, and until 1970 voting in a general election was compulsory by law.

The Upper House has 75 members elected by provincial councils for a four-year term. These councils are also elected by universal suffrage, so both houses have virtually the same political composition. The States General, the queen, and the ministers form the legislature.

Legislation is introduced by the executive to the Lower House, which can amend a bill or refuse to pass it. The Lower House may also introduce legislation, although this right is seldom exercised. Legislation passed by the Lower House goes to the Upper House, which can vote on bills but may not amend them. When a bill has passed through both houses, it goes to the monarch for assent. It becomes law only when it is signed by both the monarch and the responsible minister.

Opposite: **The facade of the public meeting hall at Delft.**

Above: **An aerial view of the Binnenhof at The Hague. The Binnenhof has been the home of the Dutch parliament since the 1500s.**

THE EXECUTIVE

After an election, the monarch appoints ministers on the recommendation of a *formateur* ("form-a-TERH"), who usually becomes the prime minister.

The new and modern complex of the Lower House of the States General.

The parties forming the new government divide the cabinet posts between them based on the number of seats they have in parliament. Ministers are not members of parliament; they have the right to speak in the States General but not to vote.

The prime minister and other ministers form the cabinet and coordinate government policy. From 1982–1994, Ruud Lubbers of the Christian Democratic Alliance was prime minister. After the most recent general election in August 1994, a new coalition government was formed from an alliance of of five political parties. The current prime minister is Wim Kok.

THE MONARCHY

The Dutch monarchy belongs to the House of Orange Nassau, which dates back to the 16th century. Its founder was Prince William of Orange.

In 1890, there was no male heir, and the throne passed to the monarch's eldest daughter, Wilhelmina. Since then, the Netherlands has had two more queens—Juliana became queen when Wilhelmina abdicated in 1948, and the present Queen Beatrix succeeded to the throne when Juliana abdicated in 1980. Queen Beatrix's eldest son, William Alexander, is the crown prince. In a political scene dominated by shifting alliances imposed by the system of proportional representation, the sovereign is the one fixed factor. The monarchy can, however, be abolished by an Act of Parliament. The Dutch would probably declare a republic if the House of Orange died out.

ATTITUDES TOWARD ROYALTY

Before her marriage, Queen Beatrix studied at Leiden University. Her marriage to the German Prince Claus von Amsberg was not popular with the older Dutch generation, who remembered the German occupation in World War II. Happily, the queen has endeared herself to the public by her egalitarianism and her conscientious dedication to her role in the national life.

Queen Beatrix and Prince Claus. The monarch's role today is mainly ceremonial. One of the most important state occasions is the opening of parliament by the queen on the third Tuesday of September each year at the *Ridderzaal* ("REE-der-zhal"), or Hall of Knights.

Although Queen Beatrix is the second wealthiest woman in Europe, lavish display of wealth is definitely not the style of the Dutch monarchy. The family is admired because its members live much like other people. The Royal Palace in Amsterdam, for example, is used only for official functions. The queen's home is not a palace but a house called *Huis den Bosch* ("HOUSE den bosh," or the House in the Woods) near The Hague.

Affection for the monarchy, however, does not mean that it is above criticism. In the 1970s, when Prince Bernhard, Queen Juliana's husband, was implicated in a business scandal, he had to withdraw from public life.

PROPORTIONAL REPRESENTATION

Many countries, such as the United States and the United Kingdom, have an electoral system under which the candidate who polls the most votes wins the election. However, this "first past the post" system is not used in the Netherlands. Instead, a system of proportional representation is used.

It is often argued that proportional representation allows for public opinion to be more fairly represented. In the Netherlands, parliamentary seats are allocated to a political party in proportion to the total number of votes the party receives in the entire election.

Elections to the Lower House of the States General (shown here) are based on proportional representation among the various political parties. There are about 40 political parties in the Netherlands, and since no single party has been able to command a majority of votes, governments are almost always coalitions. However, because consensus government is a long tradition with the Dutch, coalition governments are able to work together in the national interest.

OTHER INSTITUTIONS

Three other government institutions—the Council of State, the General Chamber of Audit, and the National Ombudsman—play an important part in Dutch public life.

The Council of State consists of the queen as president of the council, a vice-president responsible for the everyday running of the council, the crown prince, and 28 members appointed for life. The life members are chosen for their experience in administrative matters. The Council is the highest advisory body in the state and must be consulted before any legislation goes to the States General.

The General Chamber of Audit has three members and their deputies. It monitors the management of state funds. The Chamber submits an annual report to the queen and the Lower House, and this is made available to the public. Members are appointed for life and retire when they reach the age of 70 years.

In 1982, the Dutch government created the post of National Ombudsman. The word *ombudsman* ("ohm-BOODS-mahn") is of Swedish origin and means an investigator of public complaints. Accordingly, the Dutch ombudsman is an independent officer who investigates complaints made by members of the public against the executive branch. The ombudsman has wide-ranging powers to examine any aspect of the relationship of the government to the ordinary citizen.

An antigovernment demonstration in Amsterdam.

CHECKS AND BALANCES

In common with all modern democracies, the government of the Netherlands has a system of checks and balances to ensure that political power is exercised according to the law. The government is responsible to the people through their elected representatives in the States General.

The States General has three ways of checking the power of the government: first, it has the right to set a budget; second, it can set up independent inquiries on government matters; and finally, it has the right to question ministers and state secretaries about present or future policies.

PROVINCIAL GOVERNMENT

The country is divided into 12 provinces, each administered by a provincial council directly elected by residents of the province. Elections are held every four years under the system of proportional representation. The most densely populated province of South Holland has 83 members in its council, while Flevoland, with a population of only 200,000, has 43 members.

Council members elect a provincial executive from among themselves to handle day-to-day administration in the province. The chair of both the council and the executive board is called the Queen's Commissioner and is appointed by the Crown. The council chooses which of its members will represent the province in the Upper House of the States General.

The Delft Town Hall, heart of one of the Netherlands' more than 640 municipalities.

MUNICIPALITIES AND REGIONAL AUTHORITIES

Each town and village in the country has a municipal council. Council members are elected by proportional representation every four years. The largest municipal council has 45 members, and the smallest has only seven. Daily administration is the responsibility of the burgomaster (or mayor) and the aldermen. The burgomaster is appointed for six years by the queen on the recommendation of the government, and aldermen are elected from among the members of the municipal council.

In recent years, municipalities have found it increasingly beneficial to join forces in tackling common problems related to zoning, transportation, and the environment.

Police officers on duty at Dam Square, Amsterdam.

WATER CONTROL BOARDS

Water control boards, or *waterschappen* ("WAH-ter-sghap-pen"), are among the oldest democratic institutions in the Netherlands. They are responsible for managing water in the polders, and their tasks also include the construction and maintenance of roads, bridges, and other public works. Their prime role is the prevention of flooding.

Members of water boards are elected by property owners of the area in question. The most important boards are those near the sea, the major rivers, and the IJsselmeer.

THE COURTS

The Dutch legal system is relatively straightforward, and great emphasis is put on speed, simplicity, and the independence of judicial officials. Besides the subdistrict courts, district courts, courts of appeal, and the Supreme Court, specialized administrative tribunals also deal with social insurance, civil service, and other social and welfare matters. All court decisions are made by judges. The Supreme Court is responsible for deciding if the law has been properly applied.

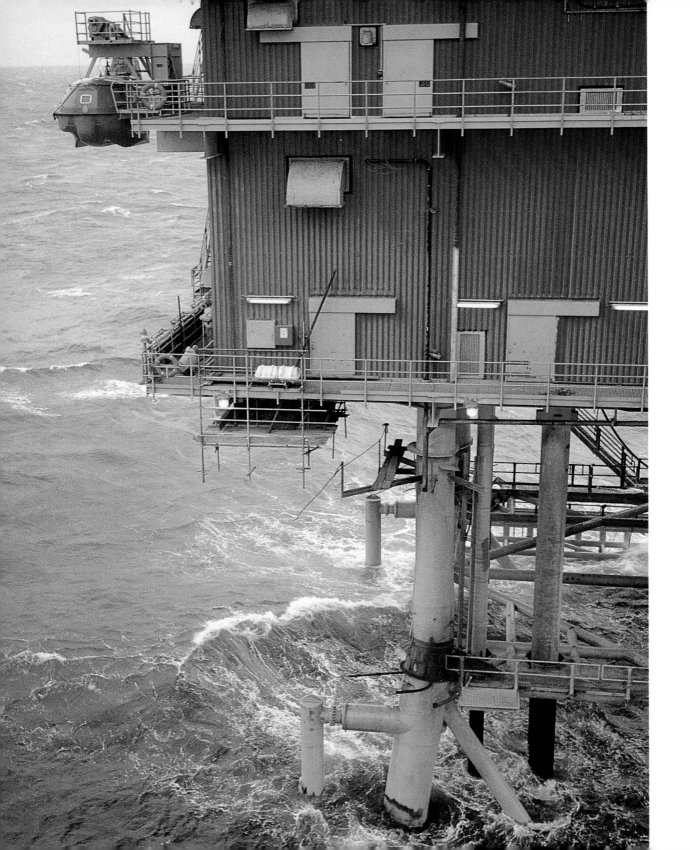

ECONOMY

THE NETHERLANDS IS A HIGHLY INDUSTRIALIZED nation, with an open, mixed economy and one of the best credit ratings in Europe. From the late 1980s to 1991, the country experienced rapid economic growth and virtually no inflation. However, the world recession in the early 1990s had a negative effect.

The Netherlands' natural resources—agricultural land, oil, and gas—are relatively few. However, its location has made it one of Europe's great trading nations. Entrepot trade—trade based on the transit of goods between Europe and the rest of the world—accounts for over half of the country's national income. Most of this trade goes through Rotterdam's Europoort, one of the busiest ports in the world.

However, the Netherlands' largest income generators are its industries. Agriculture is intensive in the dairy and arable sectors and in horticulture, but this accounts for a relatively small percentage of national income.

Opposite: **An oil rig in the North Sea. In 1993, the Netherlands produced 105 million cubic feet (3 million cubic meters) of oil.**

DIAMOND CENTER OF THE WORLD

Diamond cutting has been practiced in Amsterdam since the 16th century. The first resident diamond polisher was recorded in an Amsterdam marriage register in 1586.

Since the 19th century, Amsterdam has been known as the diamond center of the world. It was here that some of the world's largest and most famous diamonds were cut and polished—the Cullinan and the Koh-i-Nohr.

Today, Amsterdam produces 80% of the world's industrial diamonds, used for abrasive applications such as cutting tools and drills. A smaller proportion of diamonds are sold as gems. (Here a diamond polisher practices his trade.)

The Netherlands' unemployment rate is 7.5% at present, well below the average 11.3% for the European Union.

Europoort—a vast, sprawling expanse of quays, warehouses, and docks—lies downstream from Rotterdam, extending out to the Hook of Holland. Built between 1958 and 1975, the huge port covers an area of 8,900 acres (3,560 hectares). Some docks can accept ships drawing as much as 72 feet (22 m) of water. There are also five oil refineries with facilities for ocean-going tankers of up to 350,000 tons (315,000 metric tons).

TRADE

With its five seaports, six airports, 3,000 inland vessels, 7,500 road transportation companies, and extensive railway system, the Netherlands has been called the Gateway to Europe. More than one-third of all seaborne goods loaded or unloaded in European Union countries pass through the Netherlands.

Two-thirds of the Netherlands' trade is with European Union countries, mainly Germany, Belgium, France, and the United Kingdom. Industrial goods make up 70% of exports. Major exports include machinery and transport equipment (accounting for nearly one-fourth of the total), food and chemicals (together accounting for one-third), energy, and metals. Major imports are machinery and electrical equipment, food, beverages, tobacco, manufactured goods (except metals), transport equipment, and energy.

The bulk of the Netherlands' trade is handled by Rotterdam. Lying at the mouth of the Rhine's tributary, Rotterdam's Europoort is the largest human-made harbor and port complex in the world, extending for 21 miles (35 kilometers) from the city to the Hook of Holland.

TRANSPORTATION

The Netherlands has had an extensive canal system to transport goods and passengers for hundreds of years. The canal system, much widened and modernized, still handles a large volume of heavy goods—cargo can be transported along canals and rivers within the country and as far inland as Germany and Switzerland. Dutch carriers account for about half the international transport by water within the European Union. Most cargo goes by way of the Rhine River.

On the roads, Dutch haulers handle about one-third of international road freight within the European Union. In the air, the Royal Dutch Airlines (or KLM) is one of the best-known airlines in the world. The Netherlands' aircraft manufacturer—Fokker—produces mainly civil transport and small regional aircraft. It was recently taken over by a German company.

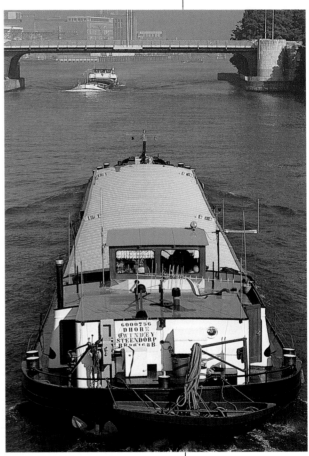

The Netherlands controls a large share of Europe's shipping, because of its location on the North Sea and on the estuaries of three major rivers—the Rhine, the Maas, and the Schelde.

TECHNOLOGY AND MANUFACTURING

Most industries are concentrated in urban centers, such as Amsterdam, Utrecht, Haarlem, Rotterdam, and The Hague. Manufactured products include textiles, synthetic fibers, chemicals, and metal products. Other important industries include transportation, agri-industrial products, petroleum products, and rubber. Since the Netherlands is an important shipping nation, shipbuilding is an important industry.

In electronics, Philips of Eindhoven is a multinational company that is world famous for manufacturing electrical and electronic products. Unilever is another well-known Dutch company, producing foods and detergents. The Royal Dutch/Shell group is one of the world's largest oil- and gas-producing companies and is also based in the Netherlands.

An electronics factory. In recent years the government has placed special emphasis on developing technology-related industries, such as electronics, biotechnology, computer products, new materials production, printing, and graphics.

ENERGY

The Netherlands has extensive oil and gas fields—nearly 22,000 square miles (57,000 sq km) in the North Sea—and is a leading producer of natural gas. Natural gas production in 1993 was 2,940 billion cubic feet (88 billion cubic meters) from mainland and offshore fields.

Although natural gas is used to produce electricity for use in 95% of all homes, over half of gas production is exported. However, the Netherlands' oil reserves are much smaller. Dutch oil wells supply 20% of domestic requirements, and the remainder has to be imported.

Until 1973, The Netherlands depended on natural gas and oil for most of its energy needs. Since then, the government has followed a policy designed to reduce dependence on imported supplies. Intensive energy-saving campaigns have been conducted, and steps have been taken to develop alternative sources of power based on wind and coal. The Dutch also have two nuclear power plants and have been discussing whether to build more.

In 1973, the global oil crisis led to an increasing interest in developing alternative sources of power. This event, along with environmental concerns, has stimulated the Dutch to develop wind turbines for generating electricity. Electricity generated by wind is not cheap, but the technology has its uses. Current plans are to increase wind energy generation by about 3,000% by the end of this century.

Tall and slim, up to 650 feet (198 m) high with rotors nearly 500 feet (152 m) in diameter, wind turbines rise high above the polders of North Holland. Most have two or three propeller-like blades.

Observers standing close by are amazed by the height of the wind turbines and the incredible speed with which the blades slice through the air.

The Amsterdam Stock Exchange is the oldest stock exchange in the world, tracing its history back to 1611.

MONEY MATTERS

The unit of currency is the *gulden* ("GHIL-den"), also known as the *florin* ("floh-REHN"). The word "florin" comes from the Italian city of Florence, where gold florins were first struck in 1252. This coin found its way to the Low Countries, where it circulated as the *gulden*, meaning "made of gold." The English name for the gulden is the guilder ("GIL-der"). It is abbreviated as "fl" or "Hfl."

The gulden is divided into 100 cents. Coins are issued in various amounts—the five-cent *stuiver* ("STY-ver"), the 10-cent *dubbeltje* ("doob-BUL-tcheh"), the 25-cent *kwartje* ("KWAR-tcheh"), the gulden, and the *rijksdaalder* ("RAYKS-dahl-der") which is 2.5 gulden. The word *daalder* ("DAHL-der") in *rijksdaalder* is related to the English "dollar" and the German *taler* ("THAH-ler").

Bank notes are issued in denominations of 5, 10, 50, 100, 250, and 1,000 gulden by the central bank—De Nederlandsche Bank. Blind people can identify the different denominations by means of a system of raised dots on the notes.

AGRICULTURE

Almost half the Netherlands' available land—five million acres—is used for agriculture. Of this, about 60% is used for livestock farming, and another 35% is used for arable farming.

Over the years, arable farming has become less important. The cultivation of crops such as rye and oats has declined, whereas that of corn for fodder has increased. Production of wheat, sugar beets, and potatoes has increased as a result of larger areas under cultivation and greater yields per acre.

Dairy farming takes place mainly in Friesland and North Holland provinces. In spite of a reduction in the number of dairy cows due to EEC quotas, improved efficiency has increased production of dairy products. With a large livestock industry—14 million pigs, five million cattle, and 90 million chickens—the Netherlands has an enormous manure problem. Almost 100 millions tons of manure—at least double that required for fertilizer—have to be disposed of every year. The remaining 50 million tons are left to seep into the ground, unfortunately reducing fertility and poisoning groundwater. This problem has yet to be resolved.

The proportion of people working in agriculture has fallen to just five percent of the work force. Most farms are small—averaging about 25 acres (10 hectares)—but they are highly mechanized and efficient in labor and land use.

Most agricultural output is exported, producing a trade balance of over seven billion dollars. Although the Netherlands produces only one percent of the world's dairy output, it is the world's largest exporter of dairy products. In 1993, exports of dairy products, especially cheese, butter, and condensed milk, brought in about four billion dollars in foreign exchange.

The Netherlands is the third largest agricultural exporter in the world after the United States and France. The Dutch have 16% of the world dairy produce market, including 27% of the cheese market and 60% of the condensed milk market.

FLOWERSHOP OF THE WORLD

Horticulture accounts for nearly 25% of revenues from agricultural exports. Most of the Netherlands' flowers are exported to the European Union.

Most flowers are cultivated under glass in the Westland area between the Hook of Holland, The Hague, and Rotterdam. In this "Glass City," as it is called, greenhouses extend for over 23,000 acres (9,000 hectares). Flowers are grown in gravel that is frequently flooded with water highly enriched with organic nutrients. Computers automatically regulate temperature and light by opening and closing vents and shutters in the roof and by switching on lights at night if necessary. They also control the water and nutrient supplies. Plants can be grown here year round.

Outdoor horticultural production concentrates on cultivating a variety of bulbs—tulips, daffodils, hyacinths, crocuses, and other species.

TULIPS

Tulips are thought to have originated in Asia. They were brought to Europe from Turkey in the mid-16th century and were cultivated in the western parts of the Netherlands.

In the 1630s, the rising demand for bulbs and the difficulties of obtaining flowers of consistent color and shape prompted a wave of wild speculation. This "tulip mania" saw prices rise dramatically, and family fortunes were both made and destroyed in the frantic trading that took place. At one point, a single white *Semper Augustus* bulb was sold for the equivalent of $5,000. After the bubble burst, prices returned to sensible levels.

The flowers and plants are sold daily at large flower auctions. One of the most famous flower auctions takes place at Aalsmeer. Over 12 million cut flowers are sold here every day.

Growers load their flowers onto trolleys, which are linked together on an automatic rail system. As each trolley comes into the auction room, a large clock on the wall is set in motion. The hand begins at a figure indicating a starting price, which is lowered as the clock hand moves round. Buyers sit at their desks with fingers poised ready to press a button that will stop the clock at a price they are prepared to pay. This requires experience and quick reactions—pressing the button too early could commit buyers to too high a price, whereas pressing it too late would mean losing the flowers.

Aalsmeer flower auction. Over two billion cut flowers and pot plants are sold here every year, many of which are exported.

FISHING

Considering the length of the Netherlands' coastline, fishing plays a small part in the country's economy. This is due largely to over-fishing in the North Sea, land reclamation, and flood prevention schemes that have cut off once-busy ports from the open sea. Even the freshwater fishing industry has declined, and famous fishing towns, such as Volendam and Marken, have come to rely on tourism rather than fishing.

DUTCH

THE NETHERLANDS TODAY HAS a population of 15.3 million, making it one of the most densely populated countries in the world, with 1,340 people per square mile. In comparison, Japan has 800 people per square mile, France has 260, and the United States has only 50.

POPULATION GROWTH AND MIGRATION

The population has grown sevenfold since the first census was taken more than 150 years ago. In 1830, the Dutch numbered only 2.6 million, but improved medical care during the second half of the 19th century led to falling mortality rates and a rise in population. This growth meant that rural areas were less able to support the increasing numbers of people.

At the end of the 19th century and in the early 20th century, migration to towns became a major feature of life. Most people moved to urban areas in North and South Holland, but after World War II, thousands of Dutch also emigrated to Canada, the United States, South Africa, Australia, and New Zealand. Later in the 1950s, as the political situation in Europe stabilized, the number of emigrants decreased. In the 1960s and 1970s, there was an influx of immigrant workers from Mediterranean countries and former Dutch colonies such as Surinam.

In the 20th century, two major population trends became evident—a falling birth rate and an ageing population. In 1900, 44% of the population were below 20, and six percent were over 64. However, by the late 1980s, the figures were 27% and 12% in these categories.

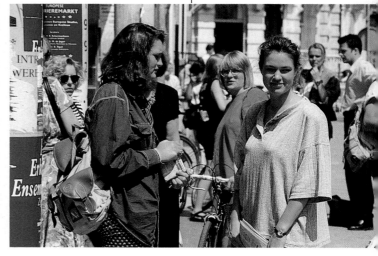

Opposite: **Children at a school playground in Utrecht.**

Below: **Two young women outside the Faculy of Letters at the University of Amsterdam.**

WHO ARE THE DUTCH?

The Dutch people are basically a Germanic people, descended from Frisians, Saxons, and Franks. They have been open to external influences for so long that many Dutch are of mixed European ancestry—French Huguenots, Salzburgers, Swiss, Portuguese Jews, and Germans.

During this century, The Netherlands' ethnic composition has been changed by immigrants from its former colonies—Surinamese from South America and Indonesians from the former Dutch East Indies. Other immigrants have come from Turkey, Morocco, Germany, Britain, and other European countries. The Dutch immigrant population numbers almost 760,000, or about five percent of the total population.

The greatest population concentration is in the three provinces of North

A Dutch Indonesian and Caucasian couple. The Netherlands' colonial history in Indonesia led to a number of Indonesians settling in the Netherlands.

Holland, South Holland, and Utrecht—nearly half of the population lives here. The least densely populated province is Flevoland, which has one-eighth the population density of South Holland.

THE DUTCH CHARACTER

Perhaps the most notable characteristics of the Dutch are their love of moderation and their respect for law and order. These values are accepted across the whole of society, from the highest to the lowest levels.

The small size of their country and their love of material possessions have forced the Dutch to be realistic about liberty and individualism. Having created a small country in which so many wish to live, they are highly organized in the way they run their private and national lives. These factors and their trading links with neighboring countries have made them practical people.

The Dutch like things to be well ordered. They feel there is a place for everything and everything has its place. This concept allows them to be law-abiding and religious on the one hand, but to accept the use of soft drugs on the other hand. They have a keen interest in small details, and in substance rather than in show. This translates into a desire to leave no stone unturned, which is why the Dutch are so good at business.

The Dutch have gained an undeserved reputation for being dull and unimaginative. They are certainly not as flamboyant as the southern Europeans, but their reliability, loyalty, and industry have stood them in good stead, and these qualities have made them the envy of Europe.

A Dutch woman in traditional dress from Zeeland province.

Opposite: **A boy wearing traditional men's dress.**

COSTUMES AND CHARACTERISTICS

Traditional costume is still worn in several towns and villages in the Netherlands. Although some people wear this on a regular basis, others only do so on high days and holidays. In the past, the number and variety of regional costumes were much higher than today, but those that remain illustrate the originality that makes Dutch local costume so attractive.

Women's costumes generally have the same basic design, consisting of a skirt, an apron, and a front-fastening jacket, often with short sleeves. Headdresses, on the other hand, vary widely, including the winged caps of the Volendam women, the silver helmets worn at Staphorst, and fitted lace caps covering the ears, which are typical of Zeeland province.

Men's traditional dress usually consists of a black jacket and trousers, enlivened by a brightly colored shirt, rows of silver buttons on the jacket, and a cotton scarf. The finishing touch may be a plain cap, a more eye-catching flat, round, black cap in Zeeland, or a military style cap in Urk.

Marken and Volendam are two villages where traditional costume is still worn on an everyday basis. Both are fishing villages on the western shores of the IJsselmeer. Since the completion of the barrier dam cutting off the

AN UNDERLYING SENSE OF FUN

Underlying the traditional Dutch virtues of hard work and soberness is a warmth and sense of fun. Practical jokes, for instance, are part and parcel of life, and the Dutch are not averse to practicing them on unsuspecting foreigners.

There is a story that during the French occupation of the country, Napoleon Bonaparte ordered that all Dutchmen should be registered by their surname. At this time, surnames were rarely used—people used their given name and added their father's given name. The Dutch were forced to comply with this ruling, but devised ridiculous surnames as a form of protest.

Some of these surnames can still be found today—for example, Naaktgeboren, meaning "born naked," Vanhetzelfde, meaning "of the same," Dodeman, or "dead man," and Grizel, or "horror"!

Zuiderzee from the North Sea, these villages have come to rely more on tourism than on fishing for their livelihood. The villagers' colorful costumes are a major attraction for visitors.

In most areas, more women than men dress in traditional regional costume. Older people are also more likely to wear traditonal costumes on a daily basis, whereas young people usually wear modern clothes.

However, clogs, or *klompen* ("KLOM-pehn"), are a different matter. Like windmills and tulips, clogs are a universally recognized symbol of the Netherlands. They are still widely used by ordinary Dutch people, both men and women, when engaged in wet and dirty work. When modern dress is exchanged for traditional costume, clogs may be replaced by black leather shoes, often with silver buckles.

A woman in Marken wearing traditional dress made of colorful chintz.

CHINTZ AND STRIPES

Chintz is a dress fabric made of cotton and printed with many colors. In the 17th century, the Dutch East India Company imported large amounts of this fabric, which became an important part of traditional dress.

Chintz is a popular dress fabric even today. At Staphorst, for example, women still wear bodices with large collars decorated with painted flowers above their black- or blue-striped skirts.

Striped patterns are also common elsewhere. In Volendam, traditional fashion calls for a black skirt with a striped apron or a striped skirt with a black apron. A shirt with a flowered design worn under a short-sleeved overblouse, generally black in color and topped with a pointed black bonnet, completes the outfit. On feast days, the black bonnet is exchanged for a tall lace cap.

In Marken, women wear a wide skirt and black apron over a striped petticoat. In summer, a red and white striped blouse is worn under a vest with a print in front. The headdress is a lace-and-cotton skullcap.

THE HEROIC AND THE INFAMOUS

Among the heroic and infamous Dutch people of the 20th century are a young girl and a woman—Anne Frank and Mata Hari.

Anne Frank (1929–1945) was a young Dutch Jewish girl who wrote a diary of her life while hiding from Nazi persecution in Amsterdam during World War II. Her family was eventually betrayed and discovered by the Nazis. Tragically, Anne died in Bergen-Belsen concentration camp when she was only 15, just a few months before the end of the war, but *The Diary of Anne Frank* continues to inspire all who live under the threat of persecution. Today, the secret annex in an Amsterdam warehouse (shown here) where her family hid for over two years is one of the city's most popular tourist attractions.

Margaretha Geertruide Zelle (1876–1917) was a courtesan and professional dancer who took the professional name Mata Hari (meaning "the eye of the day"). During World War I, she acted as a double agent for both sides, spying for the French and the Germans. In 1917 she was shot by the French for being a German spy.

THE BOY WITH HIS FINGER IN THE DIKE

There is famous story of a little Dutch boy who saved his village from flooding by putting his finger in a hole in a dyke. This stopped the water from getting through and prevented the hole from getting larger, but while waiting for help to come, the little boy died.

Surprisingly, this story did not originate in the Netherlands. It was written by a 19th-century American writer, Mary M. Dodge. Although it is fictional, the story reflects some of the characteristics associated with the Dutch. In honor of the little boy's fictional bravery, the Dutch have erected a statue of a boy putting a stone in a dike.

ERASMUS

Desiderius Erasmus, known universally as "The Prince of Humanists," was born in Rotterdam about 1466, the illegitimate son of a priest and his housekeeper. He attended a school run by the Order of the Bretheren of the Common Life—a community devoted to educating and caring for the poor and which had a large intellectual following in Europe.

Erasmus became a monk in 1488 and was ordained a priest in 1492. He studied the classics but found monastic life restrictive and became secretary to the Bishop of Cambrai in 1494. This diplomatic career did not suit him, and he went to the Sorbonne University in Paris to study theology. In Paris, he first met the humanists, whose ideas were to change his life forever.

Erasmus traveled extensively. In England, he met Sir Thomas More, author of *Utopia*, who became his best friend. He became a professor for a few years in Louvain, Belgium, and traveled between England, Switzerland, and Italy. In England, he made copies of early Greek New Testament manuscripts that eventually formed the basis of his publication of the Greek New Testament with his own Latin translation.

Erasmus finally settled in Basle, Switzerland, where he published numerous books on classical authors—some Latin and many Greek—including annotated editions of their works. His influence on Reformation philosophers and theologians was enormous. He died in 1536, a great scholar mourned by the civilized world.

"Length of life has no bearing on a man's happiness. It is how well he lived that counts."

—*Erasmus*

FAMOUS PEOPLE

For such a small country, the Netherlands has produced a surprisingly large number of famous people. Many other famous Europeans also migrated to the Netherlands because of war or persecution. They include Carl Linnaeus, the Swedish naturalist, and René Descartes, the French philosopher and mathematician.

Dutch contributions to science have been significant and far-ranging. Christiaan Huygens ("HOY-gens") not only invented the pendulum clock in 1657 but also made major advances in the study of optics. Huygens is the originator of the wave theory of light. He also invented the first successful balance spring for watches.

Zacharias Janssen made the first microscope, and Antoni van Leeuwenhoek ("LEW-en-hook") refined it in his hometown of Delft. Originally a draper, Leeuwenhoek became the first person to study microbiology by observing bacteria with a microscope. His work was instrumental in disproving the theory of spontaneous generation.

In philosophy and religion, the Netherlands is represented by several people whose works had a lasting impact on both the country and the European continent.

Thomas-à-Kempis, author of *The Imitation of Christ*, was a 15th-century Augustinian monk who lived near Zwolle in Overijssel. His writings were among the most widely read religious works of his time all over Europe.

Hugo Grotius, the famous 17th-century jurist who lived in Delft, was imprisoned for life for his involvement in a religious dispute. Thanks to the resourcefulness of his wife, however, he managed to escape from prison by hiding in a case of books and went to France, where his works on international law were published. He is considered the founder of the science of international law; he was also an accomplished theologian, statesman, and poet.

A statue of Grotius (whose real name was Huge de Groot).

BARUCH SPINOZA

Son of a Portuguese refugee, Baruch Spinoza was born in Amsterdam in 1632. His family were prosperous merchants and respected members of the Dutch Jewish community.

Spinoza challenged the value of various sacred texts, saying, for example, that there was nothing in the Bible to support the view that God has no body, that angels really exist, or that the soul is immortal. He also advanced the view that the writer of the Pentateuch—the first five books of the Bible—was clearly not well read in physics.

For his views, Spinoza was expelled from Amsterdam and eventually moved to The Hague. He advocated the rational study of the Bible, especially the application of historical methods to biblical sources. He maintained that the inspiration of the Old Testament prophets applied only to moral and theological points, and that their factual beliefs were merely those current at the time. On this basis, he claimed, for example, that many miracles would eventually be rationally explained as scientific knowledge increased over the years.

LIFESTYLE

WITH 85% OF THE PEOPLE living in towns, Dutch society is essentially an urban one despite its reputation as an agricultural nation. About five million people—nearly one-third of the total population—are concentrated in the heavily urbanized Randstad area, which encompasses Amsterdam, The Hague, Utrecht, Haarlem, Leiden, and Rotterdam.

Because the Netherlands is so small and densely populated, the Dutch have developed a well-ordered lifestyle in which allowance is made, as far as possible, for citizens to live as they please. This places a great responsibility on each individual to live and let live, and not to inconvenience others.

STANDARDS OF LIVING

Since the end of World War II, the Netherlands has become one of the most successful of the European economies, and the Dutch people have enjoyed a steady increase in their overall standard of living.

Opposite: **Country life in the farming polders. Only 15% of the people live in the countryside.**

Above: **A busy streetside café in a town.**

The Dutch standard of living is comparable to that in the United States, although some indicators put the Netherlands ahead. The Dutch have 2.5 doctors per 1,000 people, and the Americans have only 2.3. The infant mortality death rate is also better in the Netherlands—6.9 for every 1,000 births for the Dutch, but as high as 9.2 in America. However, American ownership of television sets (812 per 1,000 households) outstrips Dutch ownership (478 per 1,000 households).

HOME IS WHERE THE HEART IS

After the devastation of World War II, the Dutch faced a critical housing shortage. They began building apartment blocks but tried to limit the buildings to four or five stories, often with large picture windows overlooking communal gardens. But demand for housing was so great that they were forced to build tower blocks. By 1968, almost half of the buildings under construction had nine stories or more. Despite their best efforts to avoid this situation, many Dutch cities were eventually encircled by huge concrete suburbs.

The greatest dream of the Dutch is to have a house and garden. Family life at home is all-important, and a lot of time and effort is spent on making homes cozy and welcoming. Since Dutch families spend a great deal of time together, a home atmosphere that is *gezelligheid* ("gheh-ZEL-ligh-hayd," meaning cozy and inviting) is greatly appreciated.

However, the main obstacle to housing has always been lack of space. In the 17th century, when wealthy merchants built homes alongside the

Below: **Buying flowers at roadside stalls is part of a weekly routine for most Dutch people.**

Houseboats on a canal in Amsterdam.

Amsterdam canals, only houses that were three windows wide were allowed, so houses were made tall, narrow, and deep. Modern townhouses still tend to be tall and narrow, with steep staircases.

Dutch houses have large windows both to let in sunlight and to allow families to see what is going on outside. Many older houses have a spy mirror, called a *sponnetje* ("SPO-neh-tcheh"), bracketed onto the outside of a window frame to make it easier to look out. The Dutch do not resent people looking into their homes and, until recently, seldom drew their curtains at night.

The Dutch have always been interested in small objects and in detail. Window ledges are likely to have a row of potted plants with a variety of knickknacks—strange shells, paperweights, carvings, and mementos of far-off places. Other household ornaments include prettily framed lace pictures displayed in windows and small paintings inset in front doors.

WOMEN

A train worker.

Family life is so important to the Dutch that at one time hardly any married women went out to work. As late as 1960, only three percent of married women had a full-time job. In the past few years, the situation has changed radically, particularly since the introduction of equal pay legislation. Nevertheless, the proportion of women at work—27% of the work force—is lower than in many European countries.

On the domestic front, there have also been many changes since the end of World War II. Up until the late 1930s, a wife could not open a bank account without her husband's permission. Both men and women under 30 years of age needed their parents' consent to marry.

Social change has swept away these restrictions, although the law still prohibits one partner in a marriage from selling or letting part of their house, making excessive gifts to other people, or signing hire-purchase agreements without the other's consent. These measures are all part of a general policy that is designed to keep the family together.

Women's rights organizations have been active in the Netherlands for the past 80 years. Women won the right to vote in 1919. In the 1960s, the Dutch feminist movement, called the Dolle Minas, gained prominence in calling for greater equality. Six Dutch women in Amsterdam organized a movement to shelter battered women, called Blijf van Mijn Lijf ("blayf vahn mayn layf,"

SEX, DRUGS, AND EUTHANASIA

The Dutch try to strike a balance between personal freedom and the collective well-being. Amsterdam, for instance, is known the world over for its seedy night life—for its sex shops, brothels, and nightclubs where little is left to the imagination.

Hard drugs are illegal, but possession of soft drugs is treated more leniently. Marijuana, for instance, has been legal since the 1960s, and anyone may have 1 oz. (28 g) for personal use, although dealing is not allowed. The majority of soft drug users are tolerated, provided their actions do not infringe on the rights of others.

Although euthanasia is technically against the law, the Dutch government allows it to be practiced. However, euthanasia is only allowed to take place under very strict conditions—a terminally ill patient must make a written declaration asking for euthanasia to be performed, and two doctors must be reasonably satisfied that the patient is suffering from unbearable physical and psychological pain and that the disease is incurable. Only in these cases can euthanasia be performed.

The Netherlands' policies on these and other controversial issues are often held up as models of enlightened thinking, but it is worth noting that the Dutch themselves are acutely aware of the extra problems created by the leniency for which they are praised.

Hands Off My Body) in 1975. In 1983, an amendment to the Dutch constitution prohibited discrimination on the basis of sex. In 1985, Dutch women earned 76.8% as much as Dutch men, compared to 58.6% for women in the United States. This compared fairly well with the highest figure for Europe, 80.7% in Sweden.

An important figure in the Dutch feminist movement was Aletta Jacobs (1851–1929), who was the first woman doctor in the Netherlands. She opened the world's first birth control clinic in Amsterdam in 1882. As early as 1883, Jacobs tried to vote, to which the government responded by specifying that all voters must be male. She was a delegate to the International Congress of Women in 1916, assembled to discuss approaches to ending World War I. The Women's International League for Peace and Freedom, of which she was a founder, grew out of this congress. She campaigned against regulated prostitution and worked for shorter workdays, protective legislation for women workers, sex education, penal reform, women's suffrage, and marriage law reform.

LEARNING THE BASICS

About 70% of Dutch children go to private schools. Practically all schools, whether state or private, are coeducational.

Most schools in the Netherlands are run by private, often denominational, organizations, although there are some state schools. Full-time education is compulsory from age 5 to 16. During this period, education is free, although some schools ask parents to make a financial contribution. Primary schools are for children age 4 to 12. There are no schools for children under 4, although private play groups and nurseries are popular.

Primary school is designed to prepare children for secondary school. In the first two years, children receive lessons in reading, writing, arithmetic, and manual skills. After this, the syllabus is widened to include Dutch, mathematics, writing, history, geography, science, and social studies. In their final year, students also learn English.

Young children in school. Private and state schools are both supported by the state.

LEIDEN UNIVERSITY

The oldest university in the Netherlands is at Leiden, southwest of Amsterdam. It was founded by William of Orange in 1575.

When Leiden was attacked by the Spanish in 1574, the inhabitants opened the sluices and flooded the land. This made it possible for William to send gunboats to raise the siege. As a mark of his gratitude, he offered the inhabitants of the city either freedom from taxes or a university. They chose the university.

In the 17th century, Leiden University was famous throughout Europe as a center of theology, science, and medicine. This was largely due to Hermann Boerhaave, a professor of medicine, botany, and chemistry, who is credited with founding the modern system of medical instruction based on clinical, or "bedside," teaching.

Today, Leiden University is one of the most respected universities in the Netherlands.

SECONDARY SCHOOLS

There are three types of secondary school—general secondary school, preuniversity, and vocational secondary school. Most students at general secondary schools do not go on to university. After a four- or five-year course of studies, they either attend one of the many vocational secondary schools or go directly into industry, trade, or commerce.

Youngsters aiming for a university place generally go to preuniversity secondary schools. These offer a six-year course in preparation for entry into one of the country's eight universities or five *hogescholen* ("HO-gheh-SGHO-len"), which are equivalent to universities. All Dutch universities are financed directly by the central government, regardless of whether they are state or private organizations.

Adults, including many housewives, are increasingly interested in courses that were not previously available to them. Open Schools and the Open University have been established to cater to adult education.

CARING FOR THE SICK AND ELDERLY

Compared to many other countries, the Netherlands has excellent arrangements for health care and pensions. Medical treatment financed by an insurance system is available to all citizens at reasonable prices. For the less well-off, contributions to a state-run health insurance fund are compulsory, and 70% of the population is covered in this way. The better-off are required to take private medical insurance.

Membership in a medical insurance scheme, whether state-run or a private scheme, entitles members to free, or nearly free, medical and

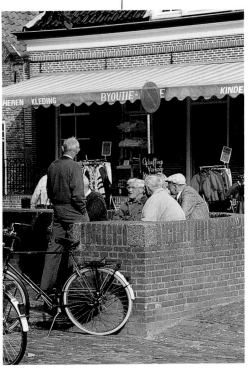

People enjoying an evening chat and stroll.

hospital treatment. Despite the extensive state involvement in the provision of these facilities, most hospitals are privately run on a denominational basis, although about one-fourth of the hospital beds in the country are in state institutions.

PROVIDING FOR RETIREMENT

Dutch workers also contribute to a state pension scheme. In some industries, membership in an additional occupational scheme may be compulsory. The retirement age is 65.

Although there have been proposals to reduce the retirement age to 63 or 62, these plans have been dropped because of the expense involved. Another benefit for retired people, the linking of pension increases to the cost of living so that when the cost of living rises pensioners receive compensatory increments, is also under threat, again because of the cost to the state.

HOFJES—QUIET HOMES FOR THE ELDERLY

The Dutch have always looked after their old, poor, and sick. In the 17th century, infirm and elderly relatives were often boarded at *hofjes* ("HOF-yehs"), institutions that are similar to alms houses.

Hofjes were built by wealthy families mainly to create peaceful homes in towns and cities for their aged relatives and employees. Many had well-tended gardens and were entirely surrounded by high walls to keep the street noises at bay. *Hofjes* frequently accommodated several people in self-contained, terraced houses in a quiet street. Many have survived the passage of time, and some are still in use today.

The problems encountered by the Netherlands with regard to health and pensions are not unique. In common with many other industrialized nations, the country has an ageing population. Average life expectancy has risen from about 50 in 1900 to around 72 for men and 79 for women at present. As a result, there are now fewer people of working age to provide for an increasing number of old people.

A number of other factors also make free medical facilities more expensive: advances in medicine, which widen the range of treatments available, and changes in the major causes of death, such as the increase in cardiovascular diseases and cancer. As a result, the Dutch welfare state is under severe financial strain and has been especially affected by the world recession in the 1990s. Despite the unpopularity of such moves, many within the government as well as other sectors of the population realize that welfare benefits may have to be reduced in order to lighten the financial load.

GETTING AROUND

The Dutch countryside is criss-crossed by numerous rivers and canals. Long before the advent of roads and railways, these waterways provided the country's first passenger transport system. An extensive railway system was built in the second half of the 19th century. The 20th century brought a comprehensive network of roads and freeways.

Since the land is so flat, there is nothing to prevent roads from being built dead straight. But for safety reasons, they are constructed with gentle bends to keep drivers awake. Bridges over the waterways are more common than tunnels. Before World War II, there was only one tunnel in the entire country—the Maas Tunnel in Rotterdam—but recently the number of tunnels has increased. They are used to carry roads below busy rivers and waterways.

Land is in such short supply that the various networks—canal, river, rail, and road—are all woven together to take up the least space possible. In towns, the roads are not laid out in a grid pattern. Narrow bridges over canals and winding streets often make driving difficult in medieval cities that have expanded haphazardly over the years.

In many rural towns and villages, the speed of through traffic is kept to an acceptable level by retaining the old cobbles that were once the most common road surface throughout the land. The cobbles cause such alarming vibrations that drivers automatically slow down.

Traveling on Amsterdam's extensive streetcar network.

LAND OF THE BICYCLE

In such a small and crowded country, it is not surprising that the official policy is to encourage the use of public transport, bicycles, and mopeds. These reduce fuel consumption and do less damage to the environment.

In crowded city centers, the bicycle is the ideal mode of transport when it is not raining. In Utrecht and around Amsterdam's railway station, hundreds of bicycles are parked every day. There are about three times as many bicycles in the Netherlands as cars, and most major roads have bicycle paths alongside. People of all classes ride bicycles—at least one prime minister and some members of the royal family have been known to cycle to work. In towns, cyclists weave deftly in and out of traffic, ringing their bells.

PUBLIC TRANSPORTATION

Public transportation is modern and efficient and carries about one billion passengers a year. A coordinated system of buses, streetcars, and trains links all towns and cities in the country.

Amsterdam and Rotterdam have subway systems, and express trains leave most large towns and cities at frequent intervals. Efficiency is helped by a unified bus and streetcar fare system, which divides the country into zones. The same tickets can be used on both urban and regional transport.

RELIGION

RELIGION HAS ALWAYS BEEN a contentious issue in Dutch society. In fact, there is an old Dutch saying that goes "One Dutchman, a theologian; two Dutchmen, a church; three Dutchmen, a schism."

Religion was one of the main causes of the Dutch revolt against Catholic Spanish rule in the 16th century. A large proportion of Dutch people has always been solidly Protestant, but a sizeable Catholic minority has always existed. Although in the past Catholicism was publicly proscribed, its adherents were permitted to worship in private. Nowadays there is no discrimination against adherents of any religion, and in fact such discrimination is illegal.

Generally most Catholics are found in the south, especially in Limburg and North Brabant provinces. Protestants are concentrated in a broad band running from southwest to northeast, from Zeeland to Groningen provinces. Some towns have both Catholic and Protestant areas. Neighboring villages can also have different faiths—Volendam, for example, is a Catholic village, while neighboring Marken is Protestant.

COMING OF CHRISTIANITY

Christianity came to the Netherlands in A.D. 690 when an Anglo-Saxon priest, Willibrord, converted the region to Christianity. He also built the two churches of St. Salvator and St. Martin in Utrecht. When these were destroyed by fire, the cathedral in Utrecht was built between 1254 and 1517 on the site of the seventh-century churches. In the Middle Ages, Utrecht was the religious center of the northern provinces.

Opposite: **One of the most famous church organs in Europe at St. Bavo Cathedral in Haarlem. It was built in 1738 and has three keyboards, 68 registers, and 5,000 pipes.**

Above: **Utrecht Cathedral. In 1579 the Reformation led to the conversion of the cathedral from Catholic to Dutch Protestant.**

71

PROTESTANTS

People coming out of a Protestant church.

Currently, Dutch Protestants mainly belong to the two reformed churches. The Reformed Church of the Netherlands (*Nederlands Hervormde Kerk* or NHK) dates back to 1619 and has about three million members. The Reformed Churches in the Netherlands (*Gereformeerd Kerken in Nederland* or GKN) was founded in 1892 and has about a million members. GKN members are more orthodox and conservative. This group is stronger in rural areas and is traditionally working class. The NHK, on the other hand, has more liberal attitudes on social issues and is more vulnerable to the modern trend toward secularization.

Membership in these churches has changed significantly in this century. In 1900, 56% of the population belonged to either the NHK or the GKN, but in 1990 it was only 28%. The figures for the NHK have fallen most dramatically, from 49% to just 20% over this period. Those who do not belong to any denomination—what the Dutch call "unchurchly"—have increased, accounting for 32% of the population in 1990, compared to two percent in 1900.

CATHOLICS AND TOLERANCE

During the Middle Ages, all of Europe was Catholic, including the Netherlands. But with the spread of the Protestant Reformation in the 16th century, Protestant beliefs and practices, especially those of the reformer John Calvin, became firmly established in the Low Countries.

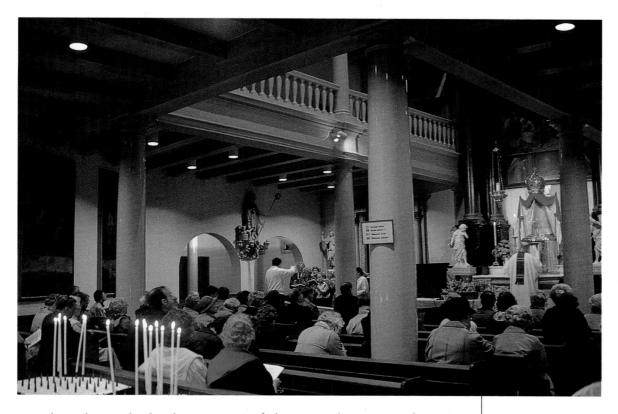

A Catholic congregation in Amsterdam.

When the Netherlands was part of the Spanish Empire, dissenting Dutch were forced to be Catholics. But after the Dutch regained independence, Calvinism was adopted as the official religion. Even so, the Dutch adopted a tolerant attitude toward other religions, and interference with private worship was rare.

In public, the prohibition against Catholicism was upheld. There were no local bishops, so Dutch Catholics were governed by a papal vicar resident in Rome. In private, however, Catholics, Jews, and others were allowed to practice their beliefs. The Dutch authorities also turned a blind eye to the presence of Catholic priests, but they did not tolerate Jesuits because Jesuits vigorously promoted Spanish interests.

The situation changed slowly over time. The Dutch Catholic hierarchy was reestablished in 1853, and by the end of the 19th century, Catholics made up one-third of the population. In the 1960s, Catholics outnumbered all the Protestant groups put together.

JANSENISTS AND OLD CATHOLICS

Two substantial Catholic splinter groups—the Jansenists and the Old Catholics—took root in the Netherlands in the 17th and 19th centuries, respectively, and have remained active on Dutch soil.

Jansenism was named after Cornelius Jansen, a Dutch professor of theology at the University of Louvain (in present day Belgium). Jansenist ideas flourished mostly in France. After a conflict with the Jesuits lasting for 100 years after Jansen's death, the sect was declared heretical by the pope. Its adherents were hunted down in France, and many fled to Holland, where they could worship in peace. There are currently about 12,000 Jansenists in the Netherlands, and they claim to have an unbroken line of bishops going back to the time of St. Peter in Rome.

The Old Catholic Church came into being as a result of the doctrine of papal infallibility promulgated by the Second Vatican Council in 1870. Many of Europe's most learned theologians and bishops found it impossible to accept this doctrine, which they said was unknown to the Church for the previous 1,800 years. They split from Rome and set up their own church—Catholic in every way except in the matter of the infallibility of the pope—and became known as the Old Catholics.

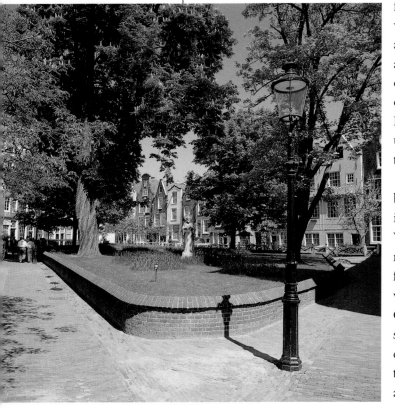

The Beguinhof in Amsterdam. Many old houses in this courtyard, which dates to the 14th century, housed *begijn* ("beh-HAYN"), women who chose to live a partial form of convent life.

OTHER RELIGIONS

Although the vast majority of people in the Netherlands are Christians, the next largest group are Muslims, who make up 3.2% of the population. These are mainly accounted for by the immigrant population of Moroccans and Turks. Hindus and Buddhists make up just 0.6% of the population. The Netherlands also has a Jewish community that is mainly concentrated in Amsterdam.

PROTESTANTISM AND CALVINISM

In 1517, Martin Luther nailed 95 "theses" to the door of Wittenburg Church in Germany. His actions started the Protestant Reformation, which changed the face of religious practices in Europe.

Luther's protests focused on doctrinal issues and on corruption within the Catholic Church. Protestantism spread quickly to the Low Countries. By about 1530, the Anabaptists—a breakaway Protestant sect—were more numerous than the Lutherans. The Anabaptists rejected the baptism of infants in favor of adult baptism and had revolutionary views on other matters. They caused an uproar by refusing to swear allegiance to the prince or to serve in the armed forces.

With the passing of time, Calvinism, a form of Protestantism advocated by John Calvin, became the dominant Protestant sect in the Netherlands. Calvin advocated that the church should have control of its own affairs and authority over its own members. He also expressed the view that a formal church was unnecessary for man's salvation—he believed that God speaks directly to man, not through the structures of the church, and freely bestows divine grace where he wishes. This does not mean, however, that the state is unnecessary. On the contrary, without it there would be anarchy.

Calvinism originated in France and spread largely because of the practice of public preaching and open-air services. By 1560, it was firmly established in the Low Countries. It appealed strongly to both the working classes and the middle classes because of its glorification of work and its emphasis on discipline. After the War of Independence with Spain, Calvinist zeal became stronger, and other religions, especially Catholicism, were forced underground.

Statue of Erasmus, the famous Dutch religious scholar who translated the New Testament from Greek into Latin.

THE PILLARIZATION OF SOCIETY

"Pillarization" or *verzuilen* ("ver-ZUEH-len") is an important factor in the structure of Dutch society.

The Dutch hold two principles very dear: first, the validity of their personal opinions, and second, the belief that different views should be given due respect. For this reason, a type of society founded on a number of "pillars" has developed, each representing different groups within the population. Each group is distinguished by a set of beliefs, and its members are organized independently of members of other pillars.

These pillars are, in a sense, the foundations of Dutch society and influence many areas of life in the Netherlands. Each pillar has its own newspapers, schools, trade unions, hospitals, football clubs, and even universities—the Protestant Free University of Amsterdam and the Catholic University of Nijmegen are two prime examples. When broadcasting started in the 1920s, there were radio stations run by the Protestant, Catholic, Socialist, and other pillars. Even today, the Dutch watch television channels still sponsored by the same organizations.

At present, there are three main pillars—Protestant, Catholic, and a third pillar that encompasses a number of neutral groups. Some people feel they can identify four or even five pillars, and many individuals may be members of two or more pillars.

POST-WAR CHANGE

The privations of World War II and the pressures of modern society have considerably altered the situation. Perhaps the biggest change has resulted from the fall in the number of churchgoers and the increase in the number of agnostics.

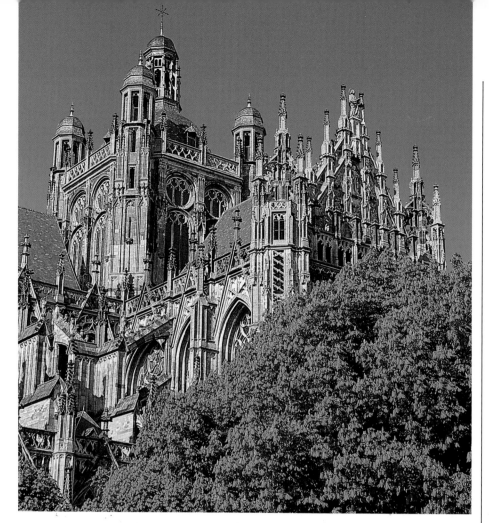

Saint John's Cathedral in 's Hertogenbosch, North Brabant.

In the past, the pillars helped maintain a stable, though perhaps inward-looking, society. In the past 30 years, however, the pillarization system has declined with loosening religious ties.

In the 1990s, the divisions within society represented by the pillars are now seen as much less important, especially in the eyes of the younger generation. Intermarriage between people of different faiths is common, and even the religion-based political parties have started to merge. The Protestant and Catholic parties united in the 1960s to form the Christian Democratic Appeal, which came to dominate the political center ground. In the cities and to some extent in the countryside, the division of society into rigid sectors has almost disappeared.

Dutch Catholics are the most liberal in Europe. In modern times, pop music and evangelical methods have been adopted to attract young people to Catholic services. Some Dutch priests have even given up celibacy—a topic hotly debated in the Catholic Church today.

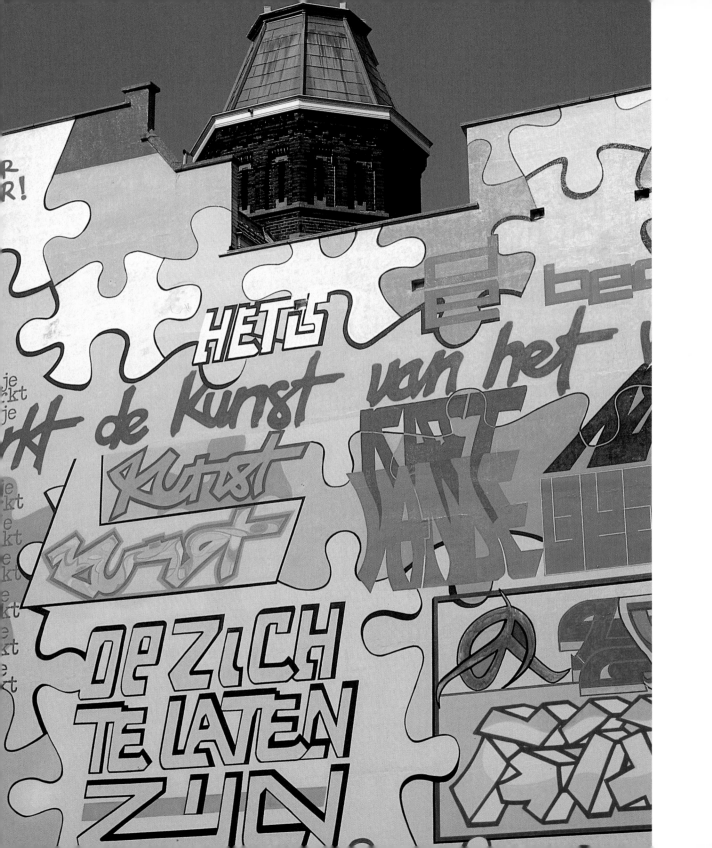

LANGUAGE

THE DUTCH LANGUAGE IS spoken all over the Netherlands, in addition to northern Belgium, where it is known as Flemish. It is also used along with native languages in the Netherlands Antilles in the Caribbean. Afrikaans, a language spoken widely by the white population in South Africa, is derived from the Dutch language. However, Afrikaans has been separated from Dutch for so long that it has developed a markedly different pronunciation and grammar.

Dutch is basically a Germanic language, and is about halfway between German and English. In common with other major languages, it has a large number of imported words, mainly from English and French. However, considering how long the Netherlands was dominated by Spain, there are remarkably few Spanish words in the language.

Many Dutch words are similar to English words, although the spelling may be different. For example, *koek* ("cook") means cook, *noord* ("nord") means north, and *straat* ("straaht") means street. *Melk* ("melk") in Dutch means milk, and *oud* ("out") and *niewe* ("neew") mean old and new.

INFLUENCE ON ENGLISH

Dutch expertise in sailing and navigation has also led to many Dutch nautical terms finding their way into the English language, such as "smuggler" and "reef." The Dutch of New Amsterdam (now New York City) also contributed words to American English—these include "boss," "waffle," "cookie," "duffle," "snoop," and "spook." Dutch immigrants in the Cape Province in South Africa contributed "commando" and "trek."

Dutch influence can also be seen in American place names—Harlem and Brooklyn in New York City are named after the towns of Haarlem in North Holland and Breukelen in Utrecht. This is hardly surprising since the Dutch were among the early European settlers of New York City.

The word "Dutch" comes from Duitch, *which was originally used to distinguish the language of ordinary people from Church Latin. In due course, "Dutch" was also used to describe the people and led to the modern German word* Deutch (as *in* Deutchland, *meaning Germany). In the 15th and 16th centuries, the English used the word "Dutch" to mean German, but it was gradually restricted to the Netherlanders and their language.*

Opposite: **Graffiti and art combined on a wall at Amsterdam University.**

Newspapers and street signs in different languages in the Netherlands.

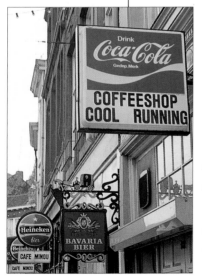

PRONUNCIATION

Although a simplified, phonetic spelling was introduced after World War II, Dutch pronunciation can still be confusing. Written Dutch looks difficult until one becomes familiar with the spelling conventions.

For example, the combination *ij* is considered a single letter in Dutch and is pronounced "eye." Words beginning with *ij* capitalize both letters, as in *IJsselmeer*. In the phone directory, *ij* is listed after the letter *y*.

The letters *ui,* as in *huis,* are pronounced like "ou" in "house." The letter *g* is pronounced "kh," a guttural sound rather like the Scottish word *loch*. The name of the famous Dutch painter Van Gogh is pronounced "van-go" in the United States, "van-goff" in Great Britain, and "van-hoch" in Dutch. Another aspect of Dutch pronunciation is that the letters *jk* are pronounced without the "j" sound but with a "y" sound—for example, the word *dijk* is pronounced "dayk."

DIALECTS AND OTHER LANGUAGES

The Netherlands has a large number of dialects, generally named after the regions in which they are spoken. The regions of Veluwe, Groningen, Drenthe, and Gelderland all have their own dialects. Frankish is spoken on the German border, and dialects of Vlaams (or Flemish) are found in the south in Brabant and Limburg. Frisian, spoken in Friesland province, is properly classified as a distinct language. It is not understood by ordinary Dutch-speaking people.

Standard Dutch is known as *Algemeen Beschaafd Nederlands* ("AHL-heh-main Behs-SHAAHFT NAY-der-lands"), meaning General Cultural Dutch. It is taught in schools and used for official purposes.

Since the Netherlands is surrounded by larger European countries, most Dutch people learn a second language. English is the most popular, followed by German and French. There is a remarkably high standard of spoken English, especially in the towns and cities. In recent years, there has been an increasing use of French words in the Netherlands. Particularly prevalent is the use of the French expression for "please," *s'il vous plait*, either spelled out or abbreviated as *svp* on public signs.

FRISIAN

Frisian is a language of Celtic origin used in Friesland, the province to the north of the IJsselmeer. It is similar to early English in many respects, and in fact, it is the closest living foreign language to English. It contains many words familiar in English—"bread" and "butter," instead of the Dutch *brood* ("brood") and *boter* ("BOH-ter").

The Frisian language is spoken by about half the province's population of 600,000 and is taught in schools as the second language. Many Frisians speak Frisian at home and Dutch at work. In the streets, a sort of "town Frisian" is used that combines Dutch and Frisian, speakers choosing words from each language to suit their immediate needs. Signposts in Friesland are frequently in both Frisian and Dutch.

The harsh, guttural "sch" sound is a particularly difficult combination of consonants. Apart from the Dutch, only the Scots can pronounce it correctly. During World War I, the name of a seaside resort, Scheveningen ("SGHAY-veh-ning-en"), was used to test whether speakers were Dutch or German. If they pronounced the sch in the typical soft German fashion, they were suspected of being German spies.

AS THE DUTCH SAY...

The Dutch have a variety of proverbs and sayings. Some are the same as in English, such as "Many hands make light work," "All cats are black in the dark," and "No smoke without fire."

Some have close English equivalents, such as:

Dutch: "Don't disturb a broody hen."
English: "Let sleeping dogs lie."

Dutch: "Carrying water to the sea."
English: "Carrying coals to Newcastle."

Dutch: "He doesn't show the back of his tongue."
English: "He plays his cards close to his chest."

A few sayings have English equivalents, but the Dutch version has its origins in situations or events known only to the Dutch. While in English we say, "The die is cast," the Dutch say somewhat mysteriously, "The bullet is through the church." Similarly, the Dutch form of "Much ado about nothing" is "Much shouting but little wool."

Some Dutch sayings do not have any obvious English equivalent. These include: "He who digs a pit for someone else will fall into it himself," "If one sheep is over the dam, more will follow," and "When the fox is preaching, farmer guard your chickens."

RADIO AND TELEVISION

Radio broadcasting started in the Netherlands in 1928. Unlike radio stations elsewhere in Europe, programing is left to private enterprise, with little or no government interference. There are five national radio stations broadcasting on AM or FM. Radio 3 is a pop station, and Radio 4 transmits only classical music. The others are mixed stations.

Radio Nederland, an independent station, is the Dutch equivalent of the Voice of America. It transmits programs in Dutch, English, Spanish, Portuguese, Indonesian, Arabic, French, Sranan Tongo (for Surinam), and Papiamento (for the Netherlands Antilles).

Television broadcasting dates from 1951, and there are currently three national channels. Dutch viewers are also able to watch programs from several surrounding countries, especially neighboring England, Germany, and Belgium. Most households are connected to the cable network, and satellite television is also gaining in popularity.

Advertising generates income for both radio and television stations. The commercials are subject to a government code to ensure they are in good taste and conform to legal requirements. Some advertising is restricted. Alcoholic drinks, for example, may only be advertised in limited circumstances, and tobacco advertising is totally prohibited.

FREEDOM OF SPEECH

Freedom of speech is one of the cornerstones of Dutch democracy, and for this reason the government encourages the expression of a wide range of opinions in the press and broadcasting organizations.

Newspapers enjoy various tax and postal concessions, and broadcasting organizations receive financial aid from the sale of licences. A Press Fund was set up in 1974 to assist newspapers and news weeklies to receive financial support from the government.

Nearly all newspapers are sold by subscription and are delivered direct to people's homes. Just a few are sold in roadside kiosks and supermarkets. Most national papers are evening papers rather than morning papers. There are about 4,000 periodicals covering all aspects of life and leisure, including radio and television guides, popular magazines, scientific and trade journals, and news weeklies.

A poster in Dutch advertising candy for children.

FORMS OF ADDRESS

The Dutch are generally informal in their dealings with one another, both in speech and in writing. Although an aristocracy still exists, it has integrated well with the rest of the population. Thus, in Great Britain, for example, one would use a title such as "Sir" or "Lord" when addressing a titled person, but in the Netherlands this is not usually so, except on the most formal of occasions.

When writing to a Dutch person, the address on the envelope includes the Dutch equivalent of "Mr." or "Mrs." "Mr." is written as *Hr*, standing for *Heer*—short for *Mijnheer* ("mehn-NEER"). For "Mrs.," the Dutch write *Mw* or *Mevr*, standing for *Mevrouw* ("mehv-FRAOW"). "Miss" is *Mejuffrouw* ("may-YOU-fraow") and is abbreviated to *Mej*. Thus, a letter to a Mr. and Mrs. Jansen (pronounced "YAHN-sen") would be addressed to *Hr & Mw Jansen*. A letter to Hr Jansen's daughter, Marieke, would be addressed to *Mej M. Jansen*.

If the precise details of a person's titles and qualifications are not known to the writer, the letters "SSTT" are sometimes added after the name of the addressee. These stand for *Salvis Titulis*, a Latin term, and indicate that the sender does not know what title or form of address to use but means no disrespect by omitting the title.

When meeting other people for the first time, the Dutch address them as *Mijnheer* and *Mevrouw*, just as we might say, "Hello, Mr. Smith." Generally, however, the Dutch prefer to be informal and quickly move on to using first names.

People exchanging greetings.

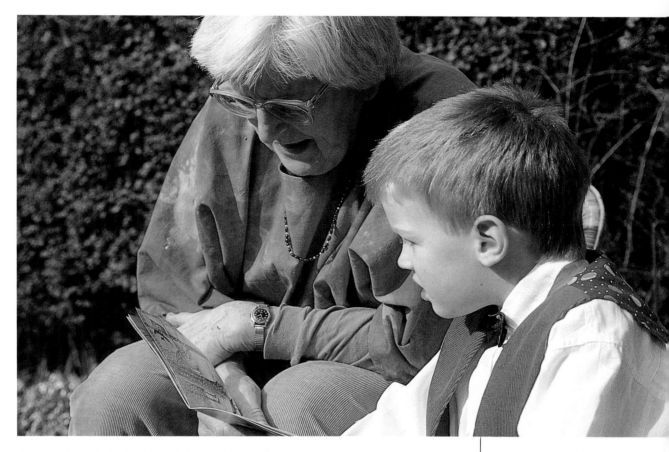

LEARNING A LITTLE DUTCH

To greet someone, the Dutch say "hallo," similar to the English "hello." Depending on the time of day, one would then say, "Goede morgen" ("HOO-deh MOR-hen," good morning), or "Goede middag" ("HOO-deh MEE-dagh," good afternoon), or "Goede avond" ("HOO-deh AH-vunt," good evening). A visitor might also hear "Goeie morgen" ("HOO-yeh MOR-hen"), "Goeie middag," or "Goeie avond," which are more colloquial ways of saying these greetings. "Aangenaam" ("AHN-heh-nam") means "pleased to meet you."

To say goodbye, one could say, "Tot volgende keer" ("toht vohl-hen-deh-KAYR," see you next time). "Dag" ("dach") also means goodbye, and "Tot ziens" ("toht-SEENS") means "See you."

A woman reading to her grandson.

ARTS

FOR SUCH A SMALL COUNTRY, the Netherlands has had a surprisingly large impact on the world of art. Old masters such as Rembrandt and Vermeer have long enjoyed international fame, while Van Gogh and Mondriaan are recognized as artists of world stature. Meanwhile, on a more popular level, M.C. Escher has achieved a cult following for his intriguing drawings and engravings, which combine science and art.

The Dutch place great importance on carrying art and culture into the community at large. Painting and sculpture are used extensively to enhance the environment. Housing estates are planned with sculptures in mind, and artists are commissioned to provide eye-catching pieces. In the development of the new town of Zoetermeer near The Hague, teams of architects, planners, sociologists, artists, and sculptors worked together to make art an integral part of daily life rather than just an accessory.

SUPPORT FOR THE ARTS

The government actively supports art and artists by subsidizing literary and artistic magazines, theater workshops, and other experimental projects. Municipal councils often commission artists to produce works for public buildings. Similarly, ballet, modern dance, and music receive substantial official sponsorship.

These policies have contributed to a resurgence of artistic activity in the past few years. Amsterdam is now one of the main artistic centers in Europe, with thousands of painters, sculptors, musicians, and writers coming together to create an atmosphere similar to that of Paris in the 1930s.

Opposite: **Traditional Dutch interior in a house in Marken.**

Below: **A clog carver at work.**

The most famous and important art museum in the country is the Rijksmuseum in Amsterdam. It contains a superb collection of art treasures by Flemish, Dutch, Italian, Spanish, and French masters from the 15th to the 19th centuries.

MASTERS OF THE GOLDEN AGE

The Dutch artistic reputation is primarily built on the genius of the great masters of the 17th century—Rembrandt van Rijn, Frans Hals, Jan Vermeer, and Jan Steen—but in addition to these giants, the Netherlands has produced a host of great painters.

The arts of the Golden Age were primarily intended to decorate the homes and celebrate the achievements of rich merchants. As a result, the subjects painted were mainly secular and provided later generations with a remarkable record of the daily life of the times. Dutch artists excelled in detailed portraits of daily life, domestic interiors, guild portraits, and landscapes to decorate the houses of the new rich.

Jan Vermeer painted quiet interior scenes with painstaking precision. Despite the simplicity of his subject matter, his use of light, of vivid tones, and of geometry and composition raised his portrayal of domestic scenes to the level of masterpieces. Paintings such as *The Kitchen Maid, The Young Woman Reading a Letter,* and *Young Girl with a Turban* are examples of his choice of subjects and skill.

Jan Steen is noted for his cheerful pictures, often of inn scenes executed with verve and delicacy and painted very much from life—Steen was an innkeeper, because he could not make a living from painting. In contrast, Jacob van Ruisdael created dark, romantic landscapes with somber clouds, gnarled forests, and ruined castles.

Group portraits of guild members, civic guards, surgeons, almshouse regents, and other dignitaries are also characteristic of this period. These were the speciality of two outstanding figures—Frans Hals and Rembrandt van Rijn. Frans Hals is remembered for magnificent canvases such as *The Banquet of the Officers of the St. George Militia of Haarlem,* as well as for smaller portraits like that of *The Jolly Toper.*

Whether he was painting individuals or groups, Rembrandt—undoubtedly one of the world's greatest artists—emphasized the human element in his portraits. In later life, he developed a taste for strong contrasts between light and shade, and painted such dramatic scenes as *The Night Watch* and *The Anatomy Lesson of Dr. Tulp.* He is also famous for his self-portraits, which show him in his youth, at the height of his career as a successful master, and later moving into a sad old age.

Most of the Netherlands' artistic treasures from this age are contained in the Rijksmuseum in Amsterdam, the Mauritshuis in The Hague, and the Frans Hals Museum in Haarlem.

Artists from before the Golden Age include Jan van Eyck, who founded the Flemish school in the 15th century, Hieronymus Bosch, known for his fantastic religious paintings, and Pieter Brueghel, who excelled in everyday scenes.

The Night Watch, one of Rembrandt's most famous paintings, hangs in the Rijksmuseum.

VAN GOGH AND MODERN ARTISTS

Vincent Van Gogh was born near Breda, North Brabant in 1853. His first pictures were painted in somber colors, but after moving to Paris in 1886 and coming into contact with the Impressionists, his pictures became more luminous and colorful.

A couple of years later, he went to Arles in southern France to shut himself away from the world and to paint undisturbed. But he was desperately lonely and under great strain, mainly because he was trying to make a living from painting to repay his brother who was supporting him. He painted frenzied wheat fields and tormented olive and cypress trees twisted by the *mistral* ("mis-TRAAHL"), a wind that blows across southern France. From time to time, he lapsed into temporary insanity and had to be hospitalized, but continued painting during lucid intervals. Tragically, in 1890, he took his own life.

Van Gogh used color and form to convey what he felt about the scene before his eyes. He distorted shapes and used color in unusual ways. He frequently applied paint in broad brush strokes, laying on the color thickly.

During his lifetime, Van Gogh only managed to sell one painting, but over a hundred years after his death, his painting *The Sunflowers* was sold for $53 million.

Willem de Kooning, a Dutchman who emigrated to the United States, was famous for his abstract expressionist paintings. Other modern painters and sculptors include Wessel Couzijn, Carel Visser, Dibbets, Ad Dekkers, Ger van Elk, and Martha Röling.

An artist with popular appeal is M.C. Escher, who has achieved a cult following for his almost surreal patterns of fish and birds and his intriguing optical illusions.

PIET MONDRIAAN

The abstract painter Piet Mondriaan was born in Amersfoort in 1872. While taking a degree in education at the insistence of his family, he experimented with painting, starting with still lifes and landscapes, often in subdued colors and on subjects chosen from his surroundings in Amsterdam.

Mondriaan moved to Paris in early 1912 after seeing some early cubist works by Picasso and Braque. There he embarked on his own cubist period, which lasted until 1917. From 1913 onward, his style became increasingly abstract but kept to the general cubist conventions of a limited range of colors and focusing interest toward the center of the picture.

In reducing the elements in his compositions still further, Mondriaan began to avoid curved lines and diagonal accents, and concentrated on using only vertical and horizontal lines. From this point, he began eliminating all pictorial matter from his paintings, leaving only the simplest of forms.

Mondriaan became the leading figure of a group of artists who called their artistic movement *de Stijl*, or the Style. Their aims were the rejection of realism and the restriction of a picture to what they considered its most basic elements of composition and color—straight lines and right angles, and the three primary colors of yellow, red, and blue along with black, white, and gray.

In 1940, Mondriaan emigrated to New York City, where he continued to develop this abstract style. His paintings represent a personal striving for beauty through extreme purity of line and simple harmony.

THEATER AND CINEMA

The Dutch are not enthusiastic theatergoers, and theater is subsidized because otherwise it could not survive. Most plays performed are translations of English, French, or German works. Similarly, most movies shown are from the United States, France, Great Britain, and Germany, with Dutch subtitles.

Both forms of entertainment suffer from a language problem—a Dutch movie or play may meet with great success at home, but it is unlikely to be noticed elsewhere because Dutch is not spoken internationally. Similarly, in Dutch literature, there are many excellent writers, but their work seldom reaches an international audience. However, some younger writers are trying to overcome the language problem by writing in English.

Modern Dutch writers include Simon Vestdijk, whose works have been translated into many languages. However, his international success has not matched his great talent.

MUSIC AND DANCE

A street musician entertains on the accordion.

Music plays a central part in Dutch life. There are few families in which no one plays an instrument or sings in a choir. In the country as a whole, just about every town has its own amateur orchestra, chamber music ensemble, or choral society. The big cities have their own symphony orchestras, and Amsterdam's Royal Concertgebouw Orchestra has achieved worldwide fame under the baton of Bernard Haitink.

Dutch composers are not well known internationally. The most famous is perhaps Jan Pieterzoon Sweelinck (1562-1621), who was an organist in Amsterdam. Modern composers who are best known outside the country are William Pijper and Henk Badings.

Unlike music, which has deep roots in Dutch society, ballet has been an established part of the Dutch cultural life for a comparatively short time. Opera still plays only a small role on the cultural scene. On the other hand, since World War II, different dance forms have become extremely popular with performers and audiences alike.

BARREL ORGANS AND CARILLONS

Such is their love of music that the Dutch contrive to have it everywhere, not just in the concert hall. On a fine day, the streets and parks are alive with its sound. Street music comes from two contrasting sources—gaudily decorated barrel organs in ordinary shopping streets and melodious carillons in municipal and ecclesiastical buildings.

With their cheerful and toe-tapping music and moving figures, the barrel organs entertain shoppers and passers-by. They are so popular that some towns retain their own barrel organs for regular use.

In contrast with the honky-tonk music of the barrel organ, the carillon with its fixed bells—sometimes as many as 50—produces a gentler kind of music. The bells were originally activated by a clockwork mechanism, but modern carillons are generally played by a *carilloneur* ("cah-ree-yon-NEUR") sitting at a keyboard.

Carillon music enjoys such a following that there has been a school for carilloneurs at Amersfoort since 1953, and there is a carillon museum at Asten, near Eindhoven.

Colorful street organs are a common sight in most towns.

The Netherlands is famous for its pottery. A product of the Golden Age, blue-and-white pottery called Delftware is still made in Delft, continuing an artistic tradition of over 300 years.

93

STYLISH URBAN ARCHITECTURE

Above: Dutch gabled houses. Gables come in many different forms—some are stepped, others bell-shaped or triangular; some are plain, and others have decorations cut into the stone facings.

Below: The famous cube houses in Rotterdam are examples of unique, modern, architectural designs in the Netherlands.

Dutch urban architecture has been famous for centuries, and in the post-war period architects have gained a wide reputation for innovation. In recent years, Dutch town planners have developed a number of interesting solutions to the problem of housing an expanding population.

The wealthy merchant classes of the Golden Age built impressive homes, but the limited space restricted both size and design. In Amsterdam, when the city's original concentric canals were under construction, the city fathers restricted the width of the canalside houses to the width of three windows. As a result, people had to build their mansions tall and deep.

At first glance, these solid buildings appear to be identical, but a closer look reveals a wealth of detail and variety. Buildings were constructed using small bricks and faced with stone—an expensive commodity because of its scarcity in the country. The houses' most eye-catching features are the traditional Dutch gables.

DUTCH FURNITURE

With the home playing such an important part in daily life, the Dutch have a taste for fine and solid furniture. In terms of design, their furniture reached its artistic peak at the end of the 16th century.

Dutch Renaissance wardrobes are among the most famous items of the period. They had four doors, were topped with a cornice sometimes carved with plants, and sat on a wide plinth. Their decorations included intricate carvings, often featuring lions, caryatids, scrolls, and various geometrical designs. Different regions produced slightly different designs. The Zeeland wardrobe, for example, was wider than it was high, while Frisian wardrobes had only two doors.

In the 17th and 18th centuries, there was a flowering of marquetry and inlay work. Ebony, tortoise-shell, ivory, and metals were inlaid into desks, writing tables, cabinets, and drawers. Today, the fine furniture of the past does not suit nor fit into smaller, modern homes, but Dutch interest in furniture design and care for attractive decoration of homes remains undimmed.

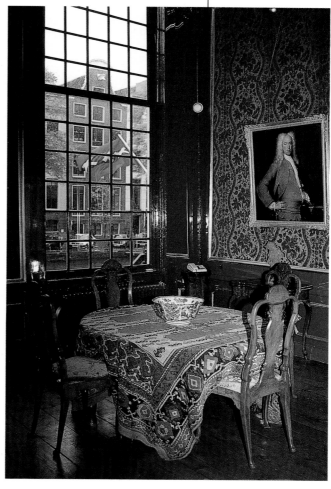

Recreation of a room in an upper-class home in the 19th century, with furniture of the period.

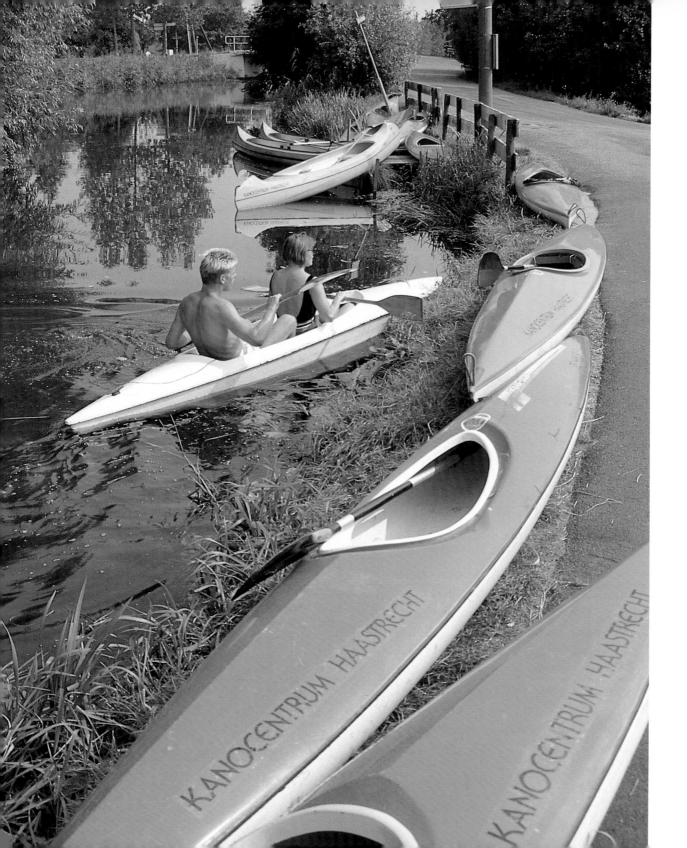

LEISURE

THE IMPORTANCE OF FAMILY LIFE and the climate combine to ensure that leisure pursuits in the Netherlands are family- and home-oriented.

In the mid 1950s, a nationwide survey found that the Dutch spent most of their spare time at home. Another survey in the 1970s found that although changes in working practices and lifestyle had increased the number of leisure hours, the Dutch still spent a lot of time at home. In the 1990s, although there is increased participation in sporting activities, led by an interest in soccer, the Dutch are still a home-loving people.

There are plenty of opportunities for organized, active recreation, such as sports. Even so, only about a quarter of all leisure time is given over to sports and much less to public entertainment, such as a visit to the theater or a dinner out.

Opposite: **Because it is cris-crossed with many canals, the Netherlands offers many opportunites for canoeing.**

Left: **A weekend outing to admire the colorful blooms at the Keukenhof Gardens.**

REST AND RELAX

Traditionally, the Dutch tend not to indulge in entertainment outside the home. Long, cold, winter evenings make a cozy home seem especially inviting. There is little incentive to venture out, and a comfortable evening at home with the newspaper, a good book, or an entertaining program on television seems inviting.

Dinner and entertainment on a barge.

After getting home from work, people sometimes relax with a *borrel* ("BOR-rohl")— a small glass of Dutch gin, drunk chilled and undiluted, but not on ice—or a sherry or beer, according to preference. After the evening meal, the family settles down to a long evening.

Nowadays, after the evening meal, younger people are likely to be out and about during the evenings, visiting friends, dancing at a disco, and enjoying themselves in a lively fashion. For their parents, the chances are that catching up on the news is the first priority. Most Dutch newspapers are evening rather than morning editions, so the usual time for that first skim through the headlines is after the evening meal rather than at breakfast.

The Dutch are great readers in other ways also. Public libraries lend millions of books per year. So many people are multilingual that bookshops carry large stocks of English, French, and German books. Bestsellers are likely to be translated and published in paperback editions.

Television is another great draw, and most households have their own set. There are plenty of channels to

Playng board games is a popular after-dinner family pastime in many Dutch homes.

choose from. Many television programs are broadcast from Great Britain, the United States, and Germany, and there is easy access to programs from neighboring European countries. However good the entertainment, many families still spend the evening just chatting, listening to music, or making music together. Friends may also drop in for a chat over a cup of tea or coffee or perhaps some cake.

Weekend activities include a shopping expedition on Saturday and a leisure excursion on Sunday. Because going to church is no longer very common, familes have outings together—a walk or a visit to a local event or a nearby museum. Weekends are also a good time to meet up with friends and relatives and have a relaxing day.

Sports are gradually playing a more important part in Dutch life compared to the turn of the century, when only 0.6% of the population took part in sports. Today, there are facilities for around 60 different sports. Nearly 30% of the total population are members of sports clubs, and at least another 30% participate in sports without being members of sports organizations.

NATIONAL SPORTS

The Dutch have long been mad about soccer, which they call *voetbal* ("VOOT-bahl"). The Royal Netherlands Football Association has almost one million members. In the 1970s, the Dutch star soccer player, Johan Cruyff, was among the most famous and talented players in the world. A number of Dutch teams rank among the best in the world—Ajax Amsterdam, Feyenoord Rotterdam, and PSV in Eindhoven have a tremendous national as well as local following. Tennis, with 500,000 players belonging to various clubs, is the second largest organized sport in the country.

The Dutch have been walking and cycling—all activities with their roots deep in the Dutch landscape and history—far longer than they have been playing soccer and tennis.

In summer, the Dutch countryside offers many opportunities for swimming, sailing, and water-skiing in specially created watersports areas, often in newly reclaimed parts of the land or on the shores of the Netherlands' numerous lakes. Towns and cities have indoor and outdoor pools, and the 150-mile (240-km) coastline along the North Sea caters to those who seek open spaces.

Clubs and sailing schools bring boating and sailing within the reach of most of the population, and there is little snobbery attached to yachting, once the sport of privileged people.

SKATING

The Dutch are great skating devotees, and even today nearly all Dutch children learn to skate. During an exceptionally cold winter—about once every five or six years—the canals freeze over, and adults and children both dust off their skates and take to the ice. Fortified by hot chocolate sold on wayside stalls, they skate on the frozen canals across the polders and around the towns. However, frozen canals are now becoming more rare, possibly due to global warming caused by the increase in "greenhouse gases," such as carbon dioxide, in the atmosphere.

When canal skating is not possible, skating enthusiasts have to make do with the many artificial ice-rinks that have been built in recent years, which are also used for speed skating, figure skating, and ice hockey.

Opposite: **Skating on frozen canals in winter, and sailing, a popular summer activity in the Netherlands' many lakes and long coastline.**

Below: **A participant in the *Ringrijden* takes aim with his lance.**

LOCAL SPORTS

Several quaint local sports have survived to the present day. The most widely known is *fierljeppen* ("feerl-YEP-pen"), or vaulting over canals or wide ditches with the help of a long pole. It is a Friesland specialty and at one time was the farmers' only means of crossing ditches and waterlogged land.

The *Ringrijden* ("RING-ray-den") is held at Middelburg in Zeeland province each August. Riders mounted on horses aim a lance at small, suspended rings. The winner of this competition receives a trophy from the queen.

VACATIONS ABROAD

The Dutch enjoy the warmth and sunshine of the Mediterranean countries, so many of them head for Spain or Italy for their vacations. With rising incomes, more Dutch people can now afford to vacation abroad. Inexpensive package tours have made dreams of sunshine-filled days come true.

Germany, France, Belgium, Luxembourg, and Great Britain also receive their share of Dutch visitors. The number of vacationers taking their cars abroad has also increased, especially when going to a neighboring country.

The seaside resort town of Scheveningen near the Hague attracts many visitors in summer.

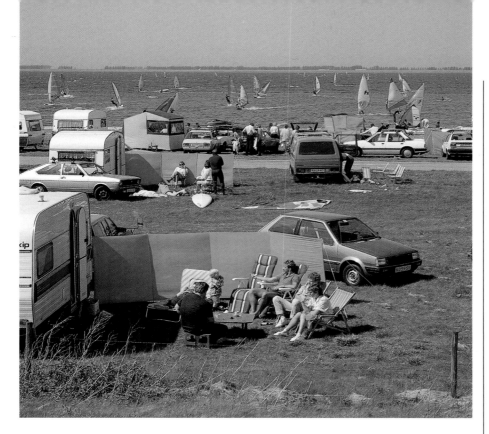

Picnics and beach sports at Grevelingendam in Zeeland province. With the construction of dams in this delta region, Zeeland's beaches have become a popular recreation area.

VACATIONS AT HOME

For every Dutch family that vacations abroad, there are just as many who stay at home. Many go for camping holidays where they can sail or swim, relax on the beach, and take life easy.

Cycling tours are common, and it is not rare to meet a family pedaling through the woods or over coastal dunes. The land is criss-crossed by bicycle paths. Many pass through pretty countryside and make cycling a pleasure. But the sun does not always shine, and cyclists frequently have to struggle against strong winds and rain blowing across the polders.

Like cycling, walking is also well organized and is served by several clubs. Real enthusiasts, of which there are many thousands, young and old, may take part in the annual four-day walking event in Nijmegen. This takes place in July and involves hikes of up to 30 miles (48 km).

Another walking possibility is *wadlopen* ("WAHD-loh-pen"), or mudwalking across the mud flats from the mainland across the Waddenzee to the West Frisian islands. This popular walk is possible only at low tide.

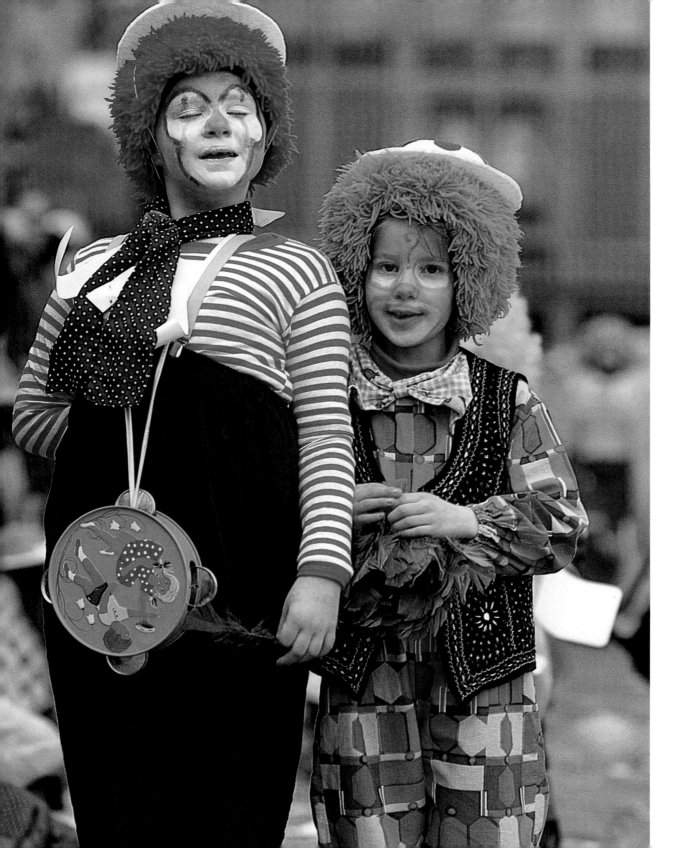

FESTIVALS

THE DUTCH CELEBRATE a variety of festivals and holidays. Some are religious festivals, some commemorate historic events, and some reflect various aspects of Dutch culture and lifestyle.

THE QUEEN'S BIRTHDAY

The Queen's Official Birthday—*Koninginnedag* ("koh-nee-HEE-neh-dagh")—on April 30 is a public holiday. It has not always been a public holiday, and it has not always been celebrated on the same date. The festivity started in 1891 when Queen Wilhelmina celebrated her first birthday as queen on her real birthday—August 31. Since this day also fell at the end of the school summer vacations, it soon became a holiday for all Dutch schoolchildren.

Wilhelmina was succeeded by Juliana in 1948, and *Koninginnedag* was moved to the new queen's real birthday—April 30. In the meantime, the floral tributes that had been offered initially to her grandmother, Queen Emma, on her birthday on August 2, had grown first into a grand parade and then into a national celebration on Queen Juliana's birthday. It also became the tradition for everyone to be given a day off work.

In 1980, when Queen Beatrix succeeded to the throne, it was decided that her mother's birthday—April 30—should be retained as the monarch's official birthday and should also be a public holiday for all citizens.

Opposite: **Clowns at the Maastricht Carnival.**

PUBLIC HOLIDAYS

January 1	New Year's Day
March/April	Good Friday
March/April	Easter Monday
April 30	The Queen's Official Birthday
May 5	Liberation Day
variable	Ascension Day
variable	Whit Monday
December 25	Christmas
December 26	Boxing Day

REMEMBRANCE AND LIBERATION

Wreaths on tombs, commemorating World War II resistance fighters.

Remembrance Day on May 4 commemorates those who died during World War II. Although this is not a public holiday, the whole country observes a two-minute silence at 8 p.m. in the evening—trains, trams, and all road traffic comes to a stop, and the whole country is at a standstill.

Just before 8 p.m., Queen Beatrix lays a wreath at the War Memorial in the Dam in front of the Royal Palace in Amsterdam. The prime minister and senior members of the government are also present.

Liberation Day on May 5 commemorates the end of the German occupation period in 1945. It is a national holiday only every five years. However, civil servants have Liberation Day as a holiday every year.

CARNIVAL IN THE SOUTH

February is carnival time, especially in southern provinces, like Limburg, which are largely Catholic. The seven weeks leading up to the start of Lent constitute the carnival season.

The tradition goes back to the 15th century, when the south was ruled by the Dukes of Burgundy, and the people of the region acquired a taste for open-air theaters, banquets, and riotous celebrations. Major carnivals

The Maastricht Carnival. People dress up in colorful costumes and take part in street parades and parties.

are held seven weeks before Easter. Some draw participants and spectators from far and wide; some are almost private affairs of interest only to residents of the town staging the event. Preparations for carnivals start many weeks in advance, and there is a great feeling of community spirit. Bands practice, songs are composed, processional floats are designed, shops are decorated, and gatherings and cook-ins enliven the cold winter days and nights.

On Carnival Day itself, the town resounds to music—in the street, in restaurants, and in the procession. Thousands of visitors throng the sidewalks to see the fun, which often verges on the outrageous. Music, dance, and colorful parades are a feature of Carnival Day. Then on the stroke of midnight, the celebrations stop and Lent begins. The contrast of the carnival feasting and merriment with the austerity of the Lenten fasting period highlights the conflict between the demands of the material world and the spiritual life.

EASTER

The Easter and Whitsun holidays usually fall in March or April each year. Devout Christians attend a church service on Good Friday evening and another on Easter Sunday.

On Easter children play games with easter eggs. Parents hide chocolate eggs and candies all over the house and garden, and children have a merry time hunting for them. In another Dutch game, called *eiertikken* ("eh-yer-TIK-ken"), children bump their decorated eggs together to see whose will break first.

CHRISTMAS AND NEW YEAR

The Christmas season runs from the feast of St. Nicholas on December 5 to Christmas Day. Until quite recently, the celebrations focused solely on Saint Nicholas, or Sinterklaas ("SIN-ter-klahs"), as the Dutch call him.

According to tradition, at the end of November, Sinterklaas leaves Spain on a boat with his Moorish attendant, Zwarte Piet ("ZWAR-teh peet," or Black Peter), who is usually represented by a white person with his or her face painted black. When Sinterklaas and Zwarte Piet arrive in Amsterdam, they are welcomed with great ceremony by the mayor. Then, seated on a white horse and dressed as a bishop, Sinterklaas leads a procession through the city.

Sinterklaas, dressed like a bishop, parades through the streets of Amsterdam.

108

Zwarte Piet distributes sweets to the children in the crowd who have been good. He also carries a cane to punish children who have been naughty during the year, but of course he never uses it.

Interestingly, the American Santa Claus was born out of the Dutch Sinterklaas. Americans learned about Sinterklaas from Dutch immigrants who brought their Christmas traditions to the United States. Since the Dutch pronunciation of Sinterklaas was difficult to grasp, in time he became known as Santa Claus. An American poet created the figure of a jolly, fat man dressed in red, and Santa Claus then became known to the rest of the world.

On the eve of St. Nicholas's Day, families gather together. The children are usually very excited, knowing that Sinterklaas has arrived in the Netherlands and will be coming to their homes. They put their shoes on the fireplace at night for their presents and also add a little gift for Sinterklaas's horse, such as a carrot or a handful of hay. During the night, gifts are put into the shoes, and the carrots and hay disappear.

Adults also join in the fun by giving each other small, sometimes humorous presents, and writing amusing poems about each other. Traditionally, the verses are supposed to be anonymous, but they are usually written by the donor of the present. It is now possible to buy ready-made poems or even hire a poet to write them. The poems are not always flattering—they tease people by referring to habits that others find annoying. But all this is lighthearted and is accepted in fun and good spirit.

Christmas Day is a quiet occasion, with a family feast featuring roast goose or turkey. Adults exchange presents on Christmas Day, whereas St. Nicholas's Day is reserved for the children. New Year's Eve is also an occasion for partying and celebrations. Church bells ring, fireworks displays take place, and in the harbors ships sound their sirens to welcome the New Year.

Speculaas ("SPAY-koo-lahs") are spicy, dark brown Christmas biscuits made in molds.

CULTURAL FESTIVALS AND FLORAL PARADES

The Netherlands enjoys a wide variety of festive events involving flowers, cheese, windmills, music and jazz, kite-flying, and many other activities. Some are staged as one-time events, but many, like the Holland Festival, take place on an annual basis. A few have long histories, but most have been created since World War II.

The Holland Festival is held every year in June and July and is an officially sponsored event. It stages plays, concerts, ballet, music, dance, and exhibitions, and draws leading international artists and groups, as well as lesser-known names from home and abroad. A deliberately progressive program distinguishes it from other European festivals.

The first Holland Festival was held in 1947, and the event came to be rated as one of the best of its kind in Europe. But living up to that kind

Right: **A car decorated with flowers and vegetables takes part in a parade.**

Left: **Poster for the Holland Festival, held mainly in Amsterdam.**

of success is a big problem, and some people feel that standards have dropped in recent years.

The North Sea Jazz Festival, held in The Hague every July, is growing more and more popular. It has been called the best jazz festival outside the United States. Utrecht has a Festival of Old Music covering music from the Middle Ages to the Romantic era.

Flower festivals continue to thrive and are always popular, as are the numerous flower parades. They are held all over the country but are mostly local affairs. August and September are the best flower-festival months, and cities and towns are filled with colorful floats, extravagantly decorated with thousands of blooms. One festival specializes in vegetables and harvest products and is especially attractive.

Processions of floats wend their way through the streets in a blaze of color, accompanied by bands, cheerleaders, and trick cyclists. Aalsmeer claims to have the largest festival. Its floats go on show on a Friday, the parade is on a Saturday, and the floats can be viewed again on Sunday. The oldest flower pageant is held at Zundert near the border with Belgium. This pageant draws many flower lovers, who come to see the best display of dahlias in the country.

Other interesting regional festivals include the International Firework Festival in The Hague in August, craft festivals, and horse fairs in different provinces.

Detail of a float in the Fruit and Vegetable Festival.

111

FOOD

NUMEROUS PICTURES painted in the 17th century reveal that winters in the Netherlands, not all that many years ago, were much harsher than they generally are today. Icy winds blew across the polders, the canals froze solid, and the Dutch put away large, hearty meals—high in fats and carbohydrates—to provide themselves with energy and keep themselves warm. Popular foods were thick pea soup, mashed vegetable dishes, and nourishing meat stews. To some extent, this tradition continues, although meals are simpler now, and portions are smaller than they were in the past.

Dutch food is plainly cooked and wholesome, with plenty of bread, vegetables, fruit, and milk products. Protein is supplied primarily by meat and fish and, of course, lots of home-produced cheese. Dutch women do not slave over hot stoves any longer than is absolutely necessary. Their cooking is geared toward dishes that are easy to prepare.

Opposite: **The Dutch are out in force each May to sample the new herring catch. Held up by its tail, the herring is eaten whole and raw, almost as soon as it is brought ashore.**

Above: **A wide variety of seafood is available.**

VEGETABLES, MEAT, AND FISH

Winter or summer vegetables abound, either grown in the fields or raised in the greenhouses that cover so much of South Holland. Dutch cooks can count on endless supplies of potatoes and curly kale, onions and carrots, spinach and peas, squash, several types of green and white beans, and a wide range of vegetables for salads. Less common items, such as asparagus, fennel, artichokes, and eggplant, are also available. There are also plentiful supplies of fish, including salmon and trout, and seafood, such as lobsters, shrimp, and scallops.

Office workers in a canteen have a light lunch of bread, cheese, and cold meats.

EATING HABITS

Breakfast (called *ontbijt,* or "ont-BAYD") is a bread-and-butter meal in the Netherlands. The table is laden with several different kinds of bread and a variety of toppings—thin slices of smoked beef or other cold meats, sausages, tinned fish, preserves, and cheese. These are used to make open sandwiches with slices of bread—from plain white loaves, golden whole wheat, heavy black rye bread, to tasty raisin and seed bread. Sometimes there may be croissants, crunchy rusks, currant rolls, and *ontbijkoek* ("ont-BAYD-kook")—a spiced bread flavored with dark brown sugar, molasses, ground cloves, cinnamon, ginger, and nutmeg.

Lunch is similar, although there may be a warm dish—perhaps a vegetable soup, an omelette, or the popular *uitsmijter* ("OUTS-may-ter"). This is an open sandwich of buttered bread generously topped with thinly sliced roast beef or ham, and crowned by two fried eggs. The name uitsmijter literally means "chucker out." It started life many years back when it was dreamed up as a farewell snack for the end of a party. A tasty and filling quick snack, it is served in lunch bars and cafés all over the Netherlands.

Lunch was formerly the main meal of the day, but with changing lifestyles and with more people working regular office hours, the Dutch now have their main meal early in the evening, around 6 or 7 o'clock. However, farmers who start work at dawn and others who find it more convenient to eat the main meal earlier do so around midday. Throughout the day, people have several breaks for tea or coffee with a biscuit or, for a special treat, a piece of cake or some chocolate.

THE MAIN MEAL OF THE DAY

The main meal of the day, whether lunch or dinner, often begins with a substantial vegetable soup. Occasionally a thinner bouillon with meatballs or noodles is served. Other starters might be fresh grapefruit or a small, cold dish.

A family having dinner.

The main course has fish or meat with vegetables. Potatoes are almost always served. The Dutch value the texture and flavor even of the plain, boiled potato and eat a lot of them with their main meal. They boil or steam potatoes with a small amount of water in a pan with a tightly fitting lid. When all the liquid has been absorbed, the potatoes are shaken in the pan until they are flaky and dry.

Mashed potatoes are prepared with milk, nutmeg, and butter or margarine, then beaten until they are white and creamy. Occasionally, they are dotted with butter and browned under the grill or in the oven. Potato salad is made with freshly boiled potatoes dressed with a mustard, onion, vinegar, and mayonnaise sauce, and garnished with chopped parsley. For something special, small pears poached in spiced red wine are a popular side dish.

Desserts tend to be fairly simple. They include fruit, ice cream, fruit pies, and bread-based puddings made with eggs and dried fruit. Pancakes are also popular and, like pies and puddings, are often served with cream.

The Dutch say Eet smakelijk *("eight SMA-keh-luck") when starting a meal, literally meaning "Enjoy your meal!"*

115

DUTCH CHEESE

Unlike Great Britain, where cheese is often eaten for dessert, cheese is an important part of breakfast and lunch in the Netherlands but seldom appears at the main meal.

The Dutch have been making cheese since time immemorial, and with modern methods, the Netherlands is now one of Europe's leading cheese makers.

Milk arriving in large road tankers at the cheese factory is held in vast stainless steel vats, where it is heated or pasteurized to kill harmful bacteria. The fat content of the milk is then reduced, sometimes by use of a centrifuge, depending on the type of cheese to be made. In the case of Gouda cheese, for example, the milk is skimmed to a fat content of 3.5%. The milk is then ready for making cheese, a process that is now controlled by computer.

The milk is transfered to a curd-making unit, in which the curd is separated from the fluid by coagulation. The whey (fluid) is sucked off, and the remaining curd is pressed into molds. Finally, it is immersed in a brine bath for several days, and then dried and packed. In a modern cheese factory, 5,000 cheeses, each weighing about 25 pounds (11 kg), can be made daily.

Some cheeses are round, others are loaf-shaped. The best-known varieties outside the Netherlands are Gouda

("HOW-dah") and Edam ("AY-dam"). Gouda is round like a cartwheel with bulging sides, and Edam cheese has a cannonball shape with a waxy red coating. This originated from the old custom of dipping the cheeses intended for export in a protective dye. Nowadays, the protective coating is often supplemented by a red cellophane wrapper.

Of the 550 million tons (495 metric tons) of cheese produced each year in the Netherlands, 98% comes from over 50 highly automated factories.

SPECIALTIES

Popular Dutch dishes include minced meatballs, beans and bacon, and chicken served with applesauce. Smoked sausage is used in *erwtensoep* ("ERT-en-soop")—a thick winter soup made from peas—or in hashes of mashed potatoes and other vegetables.

The Dutch have many tasty stews. The simplest is a combination of beef, potatoes, onions, and carrots. There is also the rich Hunter's Dish, with layers of stewed venison, sliced potato, apples, and fried onions. Sometimes it is made into a kind of pie by omitting the potato slices and replacing them with a topping of mashed potato.

Another Dutch specialty is the pancake. These are usually the size of dinner plates—about 12 inches (30 cm) in diameter—and are made with yeast. They come in two varieties— dinner pancakes served with smoked sausage or bacon, and sweet ones topped with a rich syrup, or with apples and cream or ice cream. A favorite dessert is a custard called *vla* ("vlah") that comes in several fruit flavors, chocolate, and vanilla. For other sweets and desserts, there are waffles and *poffertjes* ("POF-er-tches"). Poffertjes are small, round doughnuts without a hole or a filling, sprinkled with icing sugar.

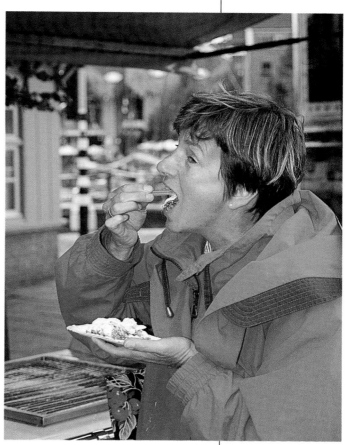

Eating *poffertjes* at a roadside stall.

DRINKS

When having a drink with Dutch people, it is customary to raise one's glass and wish them *Proost* ("prost") or *Gezondheid* ("heh-ZONT-hayt"), meaning "Your health." This is the equivalent of saying "Cheers!"

The national drink is a gin called *jenever* ("jeh-NAY-ver"), which comes in two varieties—*jonge* ("yong," or young) which is almost colorless, and *oude* ("owd," or old), which is pale yellow and stronger. Both are drunk undiluted and in small quantities. People who prefer a lighter drink have a sherry, or fruit liqueurs such as apricot or cherry brandy.

When it comes to beer, which almost everyone drinks, the most popular variety is a light brew. Some Dutch beers, such as Heineken, are sold all over the world. Wine is sometimes drunk with meals. Common after-dinner drinks include a creamy eggnog called Advocaat or a bourbon.

Relaxing in a roadside café with a drink.

SEASONAL FOODS

April is the time for plovers' eggs, young asparagus begins to appear in May, and the oyster and mussel season is from July onward. Autumn and winter bring demand for game, especially wild boar.

At the start of the herring season in spring each year, fishing boats compete to bring back the first boatload of herring. By tradition, the first barrel of new herring is always presented to the queen.

ERWTENSOEP—DUTCH PEA SOUP

This thick, rich soup is extremely filling and is a very popular dish in winter. When the soup is cold, it becomes almost solid, but it reheats well.

Ingredients:

2 cups green split peas	1 lb. (.5 kg) potatoes, peeled and sliced
3 quarts cold water	1 diced celeriac, or 2 stalks celery, diced
1/2 cup thickly cut bacon, roughly chopped	2 tbsp. chopped celery leaves
4 hot dogs, cut into chunks	2 leeks, cut into short lengths
2 chopped onions	Salt

Method:

1. Wash the peas and soak for 12 hours, unless using quick-cooking peas. Then simmer for at least two hours.
2. Add the bacon and simmer for another hour.
3. Add the vegetables and salt to taste. Continue simmering until all the vegetables are cooked and the soup is smooth and thick (about 45 minutes).
4. Add the frankfurters in the last 10 minutes.
5. Adjust seasonings and serve.

REGIONAL FOODS

Different provinces also have special dishes. In the southern Catholic areas, fish is widely served and is often eaten on Fridays. A great deal of fish and seafood is also consumed in the coastal provinces. Further inland, and especially in the northern polders where cattle, pigs, and chickens are bred, meat is eaten in larger quantities.

Specific dishes are often associated with individual towns. The people of Arnhem, for instance, have a casserole similar to Hungarian goulash. They are also known for their sausage meals eaten with raw vegetable salads, and for their fruit or rice and cream-filled pastry desserts. Another delightful dessert is The Hague Bluff. As residents of The Hague are often thought to be showing off by other Dutch people, the light and fluffy Hague Bluff—made from no more than fruit syrup, sugar, and an egg white—is associated with their elegant city.

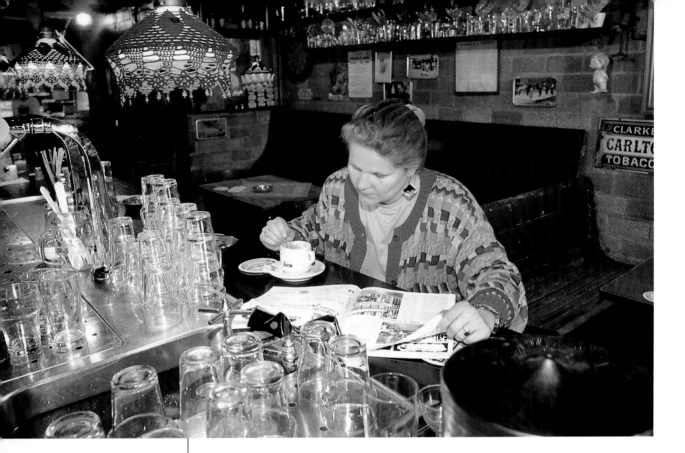

A brown café. Brown cafés have been described as a cross between a British pub and a French café. They serve inexpensive food and drink.

EATING OUT AND FAST FOOD

Sometimes pressure of work or other conditions mean that there is no time to prepare and eat food at home. This presents few problems for the Dutch, who can take their pick of cheap and tasty snacks from street stalls and cafés. If they feel like treating themselves to something exotic, then the Indonesian *rijsttafel* ("RAYS-tah-fel," meaning rice table), fits the bill.

The ever-popular uitsmijter probably comes at the top of the list of quick snacks, but it is closely followed by numerous varieties of filled *broodjes* ("BROH-tches"), or soft bread rolls. These are the Netherlands' equivalent of an American sandwich. Sandwich fillings are almost the same as those for breakfast and lunch, but sometimes with more expensive items like steak tartare, shrimp, and spiced ground beef. In the bigger towns, plain rolls are sometimes replaced by stuffed croissants.

Other fast-food snacks include French fries with mayonnaise, and pancakes garnished with bacon or ham.

A TASTE OF THE EAST

The Dutch tell a joke about one of their compatriots who complained that a restaurant had only fancy foreign food on the menu. He especially complained about the lack of good old Dutch fare like his favorite *rijsttafel*. This story illustrates the extent to which Indonesian food (such as this man's beloved rijsttafel) has been absorbed into the Netherlands.

The *rijsttafel* comprises a selection of spicy dishes served with steamed rice and accompanied by fiery *sambals* ("SAHM-bahls") and side dishes of hard-boiled eggs, shrimp, and other items. Many dishes are cooked in coconut milk, spiced with ground coriander, cumin, and yellow turmeric, and flavored with sesame oil or soy sauce. Other ingredients include pungent dried-shrimp paste and lemongrass.

A simple meal might have as few as half a dozen dishes, while a banquet could run to anywhere between 16 and 30 dishes with a selection of meat and vegetable curries.

Beef *rendang* ("REHN-dahng") is a favorite on most menus, together with *panggang* ("PAHNG-gahng," or barbecued) pork, chicken, and fish served with mild to red-hot sauces. Vegetables can be cooked in coconut milk with curry spices or served as *gado gado* ("gah-doh gah-doh"), a salad with a peanut sauce. A similar peanut sauce accompanies *satay* ("SAH-teh"), grilled meat on skewers garnished with slices of cucumber and raw onion.

An Indonesian satay seller. Immigrants from former Dutch colonies have introduced exotic, spicy dishes to the Netherlands.

A   **B**   **C**   **D**

1

NETHERLANDS ANTILLES

Aruba

Caribbean Sea

Curaçao
Willemstad

Bonaire

VENEZUELA

Anguilla

Sint Maarten

Saint-Barthélémy

Caribbean Sea

Saba

Sint Eustatius

Saint Christopher

N O R T H

S E A

2

WEST FRISIAN ISLANDS

Waddenzee

GRONINGEN

Groningen

Texel

Zuiderzee/IJsselmeer Barrier Dam

FRIESLAND

DRENTHE

Zuiderzee (IJsselmeer)

NORTH HOLLAND

Zaanstad

North Sea Canal

Haarlem

AMSTERDAM

Amstel

FLEVOLAND

IJssel

OVERIJSSEL

Enschede

Loosdrecht Lakes

Apeldoorn

Leiden

UTRECHT

Amersfoort

GELDERLAND

The Hague

Zoetermeer

Utrecht

Hook of Holland
Europoort

Nieuwe Maas

SOUTH HOLLAND

Arnhem

Lek

Waal

Prins Alexander Polder
(22 ft / 6.7 m below sea level)

Rotterdam

Nijmegen

Rhine R.

Dordrecht

3

East Schelde

ZEELAND

NORTH BRABANT

Breda

Tilburg

GERMANY

West Schelde

Schelde

Eindhoven

Maas

LIMBURG

BELGIUM

4

NETHERLANDS

Maastricht

Mt. Vaalser (1,053 ft / 332 m)

●   Capital city

●   Major town

▲   Mountain Peak

BSL   Below sea level

Feet	Meters
9,900	3,000
6,600	2,000
3,300	1,000
1,650	500
660	200
0	0
BSL	BSL

N
↑

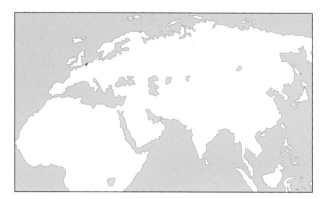

QUICK NOTES

OFFICIAL NAME
Koninkrijk der Nederlanden (The Kingdom of the Netherlands)

LAND AREA
16,620 miles (41,548 square kilometers)

POPULATION
15.3 million

CAPITAL
Amsterdam

PROVINCES
Drenthe, Flevoland, Friesland, Gelderland, Gronigen, Limburg, North Brabant, North Holland, Overijssel, South Holland, Utrecht, Zeeland

MAJOR TOWNS
Amsterdam, Rotterdam, The Hague, Utrecht, Eindhoven, Haarlem, Groningen, Leiden

HIGHEST POINT
Mt. Vaalser (1,053 feet or 332 meters)

LOWEST POINT
Prins Alexander Polder (22 feet or 6.7 meters below sea level)

MAJOR RIVERS
Rhine, Maas, Schelde

MAJOR LAKE
IJsselmeer

NATIONAL LANGUAGE
Dutch

MAJOR RELIGIONS
Dutch Protestant, Roman Catholic

CURRENCY
Gulden or *florijn* (Hfl., fl.)
Hfl. 1 = 100 cents (US$1 = Hfl. 1.91)

MAJOR EXPORTS
Machinery and transport equipment, petroleum products, dairy products, flowers and bulbs

IMPORTANT ANNIVERSARIES
Queen's Birthday (April 30)
Remembrance Day (May 4)
Liberation Day (May 5)

POLITICAL LEADERS
Ruud Lubbers, former prime minister (1982–1994)
Wim Kok, prime minister (1994–)

IMPORTANT ARTISTS, SCIENTISTS, AND PHILOSOPHERS
Frans Hals, Rembrandt van Rijn, Johannes Vermeer, Jan Steen, Jacob van Ruisdael, Vincent van Gogh, Piet Mondriaan, Maurits Escher, Christiaan Huygens, Antoni van Leewenhoek, Hermann Boerhaave, Thomas-à-Kempis, Desiderius Erasmus, Baruch Spinoza, Hugo de Groot (Grotius)

GLOSSARY

Algemeen Beschaafd Nederlands ("AHL-heh-main Behs-SHAAHFT NAY-der-lands")
The standard Dutch language that is used for official purposes and is taught in schools.

dike
A levee or river bank built of earth, used to control flooding of rivers or the sea.

Europoort ("YEW-ROH-port")
A complex of docks, berths, warehouses, and basins that line the mouth of the Niewe Maas river from Rotterdam to the North Sea. It is the world's largest port complex.

formateur ("form-a-TERH")
The Dutch prime minister, who forms the government.

gezelligheid ("gheh-ZEL-ligh-hayd")
A cozy, warm atmosphere in Dutch homes.

gracht ("grahcht")
Canal.

hofjes ("HOFF-yehs")
Homes for senior citizens.

klompen ("KLOM-pen")
Dutch clogs, still commonly worn when doing heavy or dirty work.

Mijnheer ("mehn-NEER")
Mister.

Mevrouw ("mehv-FRAOW")
Misses.

ontbijt ("ont-BAYD")
Breakfast, which is usually a meal of bread and butter.

polder ("POHL-der")
An area of low-lying land that has been reclaimed from the sea or other body of water.

Randstadt ("ROHN-stadt")
The densely populated area of North and South Holland; incorporates Amsterdam, Rotterdam, Haarlem, Utrecht, Leiden, and The Hague.

rijsttafel ("RAYS-tah-fel")
An Indonesian buffet-type meal where rice is served with many other dishes of meat, fish, and vegetables.

States General
The Dutch parliament, comprising the Upper and Lower House.

verzuilen ("ver-ZUEH-len")
The pillarization system, where people and society are distinguished by the different systems of beliefs, or pillars, to which they belong.

voetbal ("VOOT-bahl")
Soccer, the most popular sport in the Netherlands.

BIBLIOGRAPHY

Frank, Anne. *Anne Frank: The Diary of a Young Girl*, New York: Modern Library Inc., 1994.

Ian, James. *The Netherlands*. New York: F. Watts, 1990.

Lerner Publications Co. *Netherlands—in Pictures*. Minneapolis, MN: Lerner Publications Co., 1991.

Lucas, Eileen. *Vincent van Gogh*. New York: F. Watts, 1991.

Stegeren, Theo van. *The Land and People of the Netherlands*. New York: Harper Collins, 1991.

Schwartz, Gary. *Rembrandt*. New York: H.N. Abrams, 1992.

INDEX

INDEX

INDEX

PICTURE CREDITS